I0570048

VOLUME 1

LEARNING LIFE

a memoir

ADVANCE PRAISE FOR SYLVIA BAER AND
LEARNING LIFE

"I don't know how I happened to see the first of Sylvia Baer's stories that I read, but I remember what a perfect gem it seemed and how satisfying it was—like the best fiction, though it seemed to have come from real life. I was wowed by that one, but then I saw another, and another, and every one of them was rich and real, most of them pulling you back half a century or more with flawless descriptions of people so real and three-dimensional you could not help wanting to know them. But the heart of each story is the feisty, morally inquisitive little heroine, always looking for the good in people and looking for the right way to treat them, even when coming face-to-face with the prejudices or moral obtuseness of adults. She is a real-life cousin of Anne of Green Gables, and equally charming. Sometimes the stories are funny, as stories about precocious young children tend to be, and sometimes they will move you to tears. But they will always make you feel good. They will make you realize you can do anything. They will make you want to go out and make big changes in the world."

—T. N. R. Rogers, award-winning author of *Too Far From Home*

"Sylvia Baer writes of her life experiences in a style that makes the reader feel every step of her journey! She is a rare gem in the literary world!"

—Kate Hathaway, Actress, Broadway Producer

"Sylvia is the quintessential scribe of the human condition. Her personal stories of her family and growing up recall experiences that everyone can relate to. She exudes and extols everything that is noble and good in humanity. Sylvia brings out the best in people she meets and everyone she shares her stories with. Her light brightens our path. Her words lighten our loads. Her voice forges our strength. Her wisdom renews our trust in our fellow human beings. Sylvia matters."

—Bobby Manasan, Architect

"Sylvia Baer does in stories what great artists do in pictures. They break through layers of gloom and despair to make one feel what humans are capable of being—their kindness, courage, sense of justice, and above all, hope. The great psychologist Abraham Maslow would have called these stories examples of the further reaches of human nature."

—Dr. Zorana Ivcevic Pringle, Yale Center for Emotional Intelligence, Director, Creativity and Emotions Laboratory

"Sylvia's writing is incredibly lyrical and a joy to read. While some of her stories may tug at your heartstrings, they never make you sad. In fact, each has the power to motivate and inspire."

—Brenda Williams Grubisic, Retired Supervisor of Curriculum and Instruction, West Cape May School District

"It's an uncanny experience, to be scrolling over social media and suddenly see that so-and-so is friends with Sylvia Baer, only to realize that, no, they're just reposting one of Sylvia's stories again. Because Sylvia tells *those* stories—the ones you want to read and share. The ones that make you smile—often—but also the ones that make you see the world just a little bit differently than you did three minutes ago."

—Allison B. Kaufman, PhD, University of Connecticut, Lutz Children's Museum

VOLUME 1

LEARNING LIFE

a memoir

SYLVIA BAER

Copyright © 2022 by Sylvia Baer. All rights reserved.

Cover design by Semnitz.
Typesetting by Susan Gerber.

THE POEMS OF EMILY DICKINSON, edited by Thomas H. Johnson, Cambridge, Mass.: The Belknap Press of Harvard University Press, Copyright © 1951, 1955 by the President and Fellows of Harvard College. Copyright © renewed 1979, 1983 by the President and Fellows of Harvard College. Copyright © 1914, 1918, 1919, 1924, 1929, 1930, 1932, 1935, 1937, 1942, by Martha Dickinson Bianchi. Copyright © 1952, 1957, 1958, 1963, 1965, by Mary L. Hampson. Used by permission. All rights reserved.

No part of this book may be reproduced, stored, or transmitted in any form or by any means except by the prior written permission of the author, except for reviewers who may quote brief excerpts in conjunction with an article in a magazine, newspaper, blog, or other publication. While the author has used her best efforts in preparing this book she makes no representations or warranties with respect to the accuracy of completeness of its contents. The author specifically disclaims any implied warranty of merchantability or fitness for a particular purpose, and no warranty may be created or extended by a sales representative or retailer, or via written sales materials.

For media inquiries, questions about bulk purchases, permission to use any of the content of this book, or speaking availability, please visit www.sylviabaerwrites.com.

Library of Congress CIP is on file.

ISBN 979-8-9864361-0-4 (hardcover)
ISBN 979-8-9864361-1-1 (paperback)
ISBN 979-8-9864361-2-8 (ebook)

This book is dedicated to John Baer,
whose steadfast inner light brilliantly illuminates every aspect
of our shared life. He is a gift to me and to the world.

CONTENTS

I am out with lanterns, looking for myself.

—*Emily Dickinson*

NOTE TO THE READER:
There are several Dickinson poems scattered throughout this book. They have taken root in my heart and mind, and they have enriched my stories. Perhaps you, too, will find them enlightening.

PREFACE

Winds carry seeds to places unknown, where they will bury themselves deep in some new soil and wait patiently for the perfect time to rise—"Scarlet Freight," according to one of my favorite poets, Emily Dickinson. Plants seem to have a special magic. From the first time my grandmother taught me how to plant, water, feed, and protect seeds, I've been enchanted by them. I've named trees (Jeffrey, Samantha, Jordan), considered peonies (Latia, the bright ruffled pink one; Madeline, the yellow lemony-scented one) my close personal friends, and had almost sacred connections with tomatoes. So simple a thing to watch a plant grow, and yet so mysterious, especially the way each one has the potential of creating another.

Such, I envision, are the stories you hold in your hands right now. Each one has its own life, but within it is a seed that might find gentle conditions for growth within your own world. Like the names I have given my trees and flowers, the names of the people in this book have been changed out of respect for the privacy of those individuals and their families. The names of my own relatives have stayed. The events and the encounters herein are all true, with a little staking here or a bit of pruning there. They are parts of my life. Small things, really. Just seedlings. May the warmth of your kind reception and the nutrients of your own shared experiences help them to flourish.

HOW MANY FLOWERS FAIL IN WOOD—
Emily Dickinson

How many Flowers fail in Wood—
Or perish from the Hill—
Without the privilege to know
That they are Beautiful—

How many cast a nameless Pod
Upon the nearest Breeze—
Unconscious of the Scarlet Freight—
It bear to other eyes—

F534 (1863) J40

Sylvia Baer
April 2022

Emily Dickinson: 1203

The Past is such a curious Creature
To look her in the Face
A Transport may receipt us
Or a Disgrace—

Unarmed if any meet her
I charge him fly
Her faded Ammunition
Might yet reply.

WHO WILL TELL OUR STORIES?

When I walked in, she was on the sofa crying. "There's no hope for any of us," my mother spurted out between sobs. Just then my father came into the room with a glass of water and two aspirin.

"Here, Sara, take these. It will help." She looked up at him gratefully and swallowed the pills.

"Mom, what happened?" I asked.

"Jaqueline Kennedy Onassis has just died. Died," she answered as she set the glass down and began leaving the room. "And I'm going to lie down for a bit."

It was May 19, 1994, I was forty-four years old, and my father and I were left to sort out the pieces of my mother's grief. "I don't really understand it, Daddy," I began. "I mean, she hasn't met the woman. She only knows her through stories in the paper and magazines and TV. Why is she so emotional?"

Equally baffled, my father posed some possibilities. "Well, they're close to the same age. And maybe she's afraid that if someone with so much power and money and connections can die, then, well . . ." Here he trailed off, afraid to finish the sentence. But then looked me squarely in the face and did: "We can all die. We will all die. It's a hard reality at our age and a sad, but inevitable, truth."

"You know," he continued, "Jackie was beautiful and elegant, but your mother was so much more so. When I first met her, I thought she was the most glamorous woman I had ever known. She still is, you know," he sighed. I had never really thought about their first meetings. Fresh out of a New York University master's program in economics, my American father had gone to Montevideo, Uruguay, to start a branch of the Schick razor company. He was twenty-five years old. He spoke little Spanish and knew right away he needed help with not only the language but also the customs of the country.

"When she walked into my office I found it hard to say anything. Her raven-black hair fell in waves on her shoulders and when she reached out her white-gloved hand to take mine, I knew I was a goner." He laughed, remembering the details. "She didn't seem like she had much experience as a secretary and really, after she started working, she was abysmal at it. Tried firing her twice, but she wouldn't stay away and neither could I. When we formally became a couple, I was finally able to meet her three-year-old daughter, you," he smiled, "and I loved you from the first moment as well." He hugged me and continued, "You know she had been in medical school but then stopped. She married Harry and you were born and then Harry was horrible to both of you. When he disappeared, everyone was relieved. And then we met, fell in love, got married, and moved here to the U.S."

It seemed so simple when he told it. But I knew there was more.

Now she came back into the living room, her eyes red and puffy, a tissue clutched in her hand, and sat down next to me. My father took this as a cue to leave us alone and wandered off into the kitchen. "I want to explain," she began, "what troubles me so much. Jackie Kennedy Onassis was a really complicated woman. She had a hard life."

I jumped in, "Sure. Her husband was president and then he was assassinated in the car, right next to her."

Now my mother continued, "Well, of course there was that terrible trauma. But, she was full of so many tragedies. She had miscarriages, and her husband had so many affairs. He was terrible to her. She only married him because everyone said that since she was already in her twenties she was getting very old and needed to find a husband soon. She had gone to college and had earned a job at a magazine, but was told she really should just get married. I understand this. It was like that in those days."

Now she sipped the water she'd left behind, and I noticed a hint of her newly applied lipstick on the rim. Even in her sadness my mother wanted to look "put-together" as she called it. "So she married JFK, helped him become president, had two children, and when he died, she was alone. Alone. All that wealth and popularity and beauty, and still alone."

"But then she married one of the richest men in the world, right?" I said.

She continued, "Who knows why she did that? Maybe she loved him. Maybe she saw no choice. Maybe she was lonely. Maybe it was security. But that too wasn't happy."

Now she looked at the large clock on the wall and fell silent. We could hear it tick, tick, tick the seconds away.

She looked at me again. "When he died, she came back to the U.S. She began working with the arts and with publishing. You know, the press was not kind to her. But she kept going. Kept going. Until today." Now my mother's head folded down into her hands.

"Mom," I said as I put my arm around her shoulder, "is it upsetting to you that if she can die, we all can? I'm trying to understand."

"No, it's not really that," she said as her tear-filled eyes searched mine. "It's her story. Who tells her story now? How will we know about her life, her struggles, her energies?"

Maybe my mother had a sense then that her arteries were starting their hardening, her heart beating out a new staccato rhythm, not allowing enough oxygen for her brain to connect the wandering memories. "Sylvia," she continued, "I'm afraid that all our own stories will be lost. What will happen to all of the life we led? Where will it go?"

I gently put my hand on her quivering, rounded back and said, "Tell me about the time you and father got the car stuck in the thick mud on your way to Brazil," making us both chuckle at the memory of an old family tale. Then we got out photo albums and talked over tea. My father grilled some

4

steaks and we kept talking over dinner. And into the chill of the May night we laughed.

Five years later, my father died of cancer. Five years after that my mother died of her heart conditions. And today I am here right now telling you, dear readers, their stories—keeping them alive.

U.S. Embassy 4th of July
Montreal 1952

NEEDLES

"What's the point of being sad about life," she would tell me in 1974 when in her eighties she sat with me, stitching yet another piece of cloth (red taffeta this time) which she rescued from some trash bin somewhere and was now resurrecting into an elegant dinner ensemble. Her agile fingers played hide-and-seek with the quick needle as the thread dangled and swayed over and under her creation. We were talking about life in the living room of my newly built first home where she'd come from very far away to stay with me for a few weeks. I knew the essence of so many family stories, but I wanted, now, to know how she actually felt about things.

In 1918 my grandmother worked as a hat model in Warsaw, Poland, to pay for her tuition in the university which she attended without her father's knowledge. ("Stop reading so much. Women are not meant for that.") She wanted dearly to attend the medical school, but as a woman she was not allowed. And when her father found out about her studies he was outraged and forced her to marry a man who would later turn out to be a scoundrel and would steal everything from her—twice. Before her father's demand, she had had a wild love affair with a dashing Russian soldier who she told me was the love of her life. Later, right before WWII, she immigrated to the safety of the South American country of Uruguay with her two small children in tow, no money, and no knowledge of the Spanish language. To feed the children, she designed hats—she knew about them from her modeling days. Her charm and beauty helped make her business profitable. But her husband found her and twice more he stole all she had.

Over tea and cakes and chocolates with threads and fabric spread out around us, the bright sunlight streaming through the windows making changing shadows on the walls, we passed many afternoons. I tried to sew with her, but my skills seemed hopeless. She patted my knee in support and said, "Ah, Sylvia, your needle is a pen. You write so much—I think maybe you stitch stories together one day—Maybe like a beautiful blanket of memories you can wrap around you on bright or dark days."

I smiled and nodded. "You know," I said, "I don't think I've ever heard you complain about your life. Not once."

She smiled, "It's life. You take what you can find and, see, like this skirt, you can throw it out, you can curse the frayed edges, or you can take a needle in your hand and make something beautiful and useful." Her eyes twinkled as her fingers nimbly made a future.

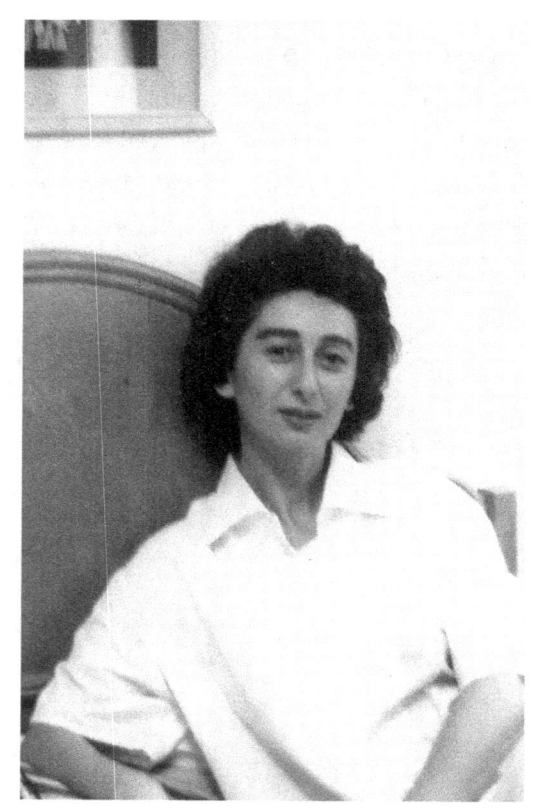

CHAPTER 1

MY TWO BIRTH DATES

"Oh, he was a good man. He didn't deserve that terrible son he had. Terrible." It was summer 1967 and I had just graduated from high school. My mother, her mother (my grandmother Margot), and I were going over some family photos. Somehow my transition from one phase of life to another, a more adult one, stirred a sudden need in me to understand more about my past. I had heard many of the stories, but when I asked more specifically about the day I was born, and why I had always had two birthdays, the two women, who had been chatting amiably, became more solemn.

My grandmother sighed and almost hissed out his name, "Harry Meindl, your mother's first husband—your biological father, he disappeared, and his father, Max, went out to try to find him." Ah, she was talking about my grandfather Meindl, a man I adored and who I'd had to leave behind in Uruguay in 1957 when my new American father—my real father—and my mom and I moved to the United States. She continued, "He looked everywhere, but with no luck.

"And then you were born, on January 27th.

"You were such a beautiful little baby, and when Max first saw you, you smiled at him. He knew that newborns don't smile intentionally, but he looked in your eyes and you looked back and smiled. I was there. I know you meant it." Now I smiled at her as she continued and my mother, listening and nodding, wiped away some memory-tears. "So your grandfather vowed to find Harry. Vowed to make things right."

Now I interrupted. This was a part of the story I never fully understood. "Why was it so important? I mean Harry was a horrible man to leave like that. Why was it so necessary to find him?"

My mother sighed and took over the story. "In Uruguay in 1950 when a baby was born the birth certificate had to be signed by the father. That was the law."

Now I became outraged, "What? That's absurd! A baby is born—what does it matter?"

After my short outburst, my mother continued, "Like it or not, that was the law. So Max was hell-bent on finding Harry so your birth could be . . . umm . . . legal." Her voice quivered a bit and my grandmother continued for her.

"There was a two-day grace period to find the father, but by January 29th he had still not been found. Your grandfather convinced the authorities to push the time two more days. But by January 31st it was too late. Max was broken-hearted. The officials brought him the document and he couldn't sign it. He wept. He couldn't sign it."

Now my mother was crying but my grandmother sat up taller and, steely-eyed, kept going, "So I told them to give me the paper and I would sign it." I wasn't quite sure why there was such a fuss. It was just a signature. My grandmother continued, "You see, with no father to sign, we couldn't sign at the top. We had to sign at the bottom where it says 'bastarda,' bastard. And because of the extra two days we had to change your birthday to the 29th."

Now my mother had collected herself and actually started to laugh. "Oh Sylvia. You should have heard your grandmother after she signed it."

They both started laughing as she continued, "She started calling all of the men in that government office names and then declared that if her granddaughter was going to be labeled a bastarda that term was too good for them and their ridiculous laws. Even Max started to laugh when he heard her tirade."

Now, in 1967, we three women were laughing—the two of them remembering, and me picturing that scene. Just at that moment Fred Kuhner, who became my real father from the time he married my mother in 1954, well before he was able to legally adopt me in the United States in 1958, walked into the room.

"What's all the hilarity about?" he asked.

"Oh, Daddy, they're telling me details about my birthdays—both of them."

He smiled and said, "Well, when I adopted you at the Passaic County, New Jersey, courthouse we had to use your bureaucratic birth date, January 29th, on the official papers. And since the day I adopted you was one of the best days of my life, I honor that day because it gave me you." And he hugged me.

My grandmother now looked at me and forcefully said, "You see, Sylvia, what gives legitimacy to life? No paper. No document. This"—she swept her arm around to include us all—"it's love."

CHAPTER 2

FROM VIOLENCE

"Yes, it was all true. We actually heard it from Harry in the police station before he disappeared." My grandmother had been sitting with my mother and I, drinking tea and nibbling some butter cookies. It was 1965 and I was getting ready to go back to my New England prep school. My last suitcase was packed and tomorrow we'd drive the five hours from the city to the hills of Western Massachusetts.

"Are you nervous?" my mom asked.

"Nope—excited to start my junior year! Can't wait!" I replied.

She sighed and looked at her own mother and exclaimed, "Tenacious. That's what she is. Tenacious. Never gives up." My grandmother let out a sad, wistful, soft laugh and said, "She was like that from the beginning, remember?" They looked at each other knowingly and she continued recounting a story I had only heard parts of before. Now she told it all.

Before she married my father, my mother was married to Harry. Harry was, by all accounts, an incredibly handsome and charismatic man. His parents came from a very well-connected family in Czechoslovakia with ties to royalty.

When because of the Nazis and the impending takeover they had to suddenly immigrate to the small country of Uruguay in South America, they could take very little. Harry was a teenager at the time and resented this. He tried to reconcile himself to the new world he was plunked down in, but it did not work. He became involved in gambling and drinking and drugs. But he was able to talk his way out of a great deal because of his charm.

My mother met him one afternoon at a local café and was swept off her feet. She knew nothing of his other side. He talked a good game about investing and business deals, and she believed him. For her part, my mom was a gorgeous, Hollywood-like beauty with seductive good looks and genuine gullibility.

After they were married a short time, his veneer began to wear off. He'd be gone for days at a time on vague "business trips" with unclear destinations and timelines.

She sought solace at his parents' home where their genuine kindness and love comforted her and provided some guidance and understanding. They were not optimistic. They tried to warn her, knowing full well the pain of loving him.

When his abusive behavior began its cycle of torment, denial, pain, and grief, she thought she was done. But like so many women before her and after, time after time she took him back. She became pregnant and almost lost the baby several times. But after a multi-month bed rest, a little girl was born who almost died during and right after birth, but then gained strength.

Things seemed fine for a few months. ("Yes, this is all true," my grandmother interjected in this story, although I had heard enough parts of it before to know that.) And then it fell apart.

One night, waking to an eerily quiet room, my mother found Harry bending over their two-month-old baby girl's crib, strangling her. "She cries too much," he started yelling while my mother threw a lamp at him, grabbed the baby, and ran shoeless to the nearest hospital.

"They said it was some sort of miracle," my mother stated simply, and continued: "A miracle. With that kind of force, anyone else would have succumbed." She set down her teacup neatly in its saucer and reached for my left hand, while my grandmother took my right, and said, "I knew from before you were born how strong you would be. He could not strangle the life force in you. Your voice will always be heard."

After a night in the hospital my mother and I moved in with my grandmother and Harry disappeared. His parents, who I adored, also helped to raise me. Three years later my mother married Fred Kuhner, the man who would always be my real father—the man who I loved with all my heart and who celebrated and encouraged my voice and also my tenacity.

Even in 1965, even at fifteen years of age, I knew my story had a long and curious road behind and ahead. I was right.

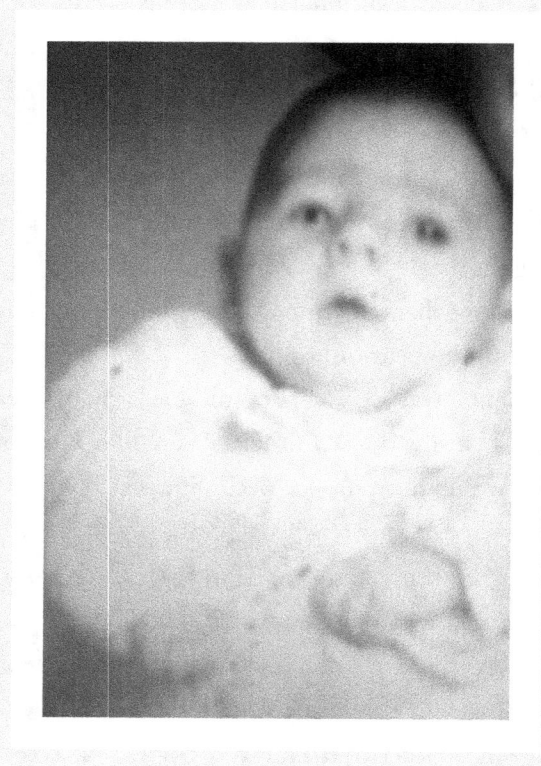

EMILY DICKINSON: 451

The Outer—from the Inner
Derives its Magnitude—
'Tis Duke, or Dwarf, according
As is the Central Mood—

The fine—unvarying Axis
That regulates the Wheel—
Though Spokes—spin—more conspicuous
And fling a dust—the while.

The Inner—paints the Outer—
The Brush without the Hand—
Its Picture publishes—precise—
As is the inner Brand—

On fine—Arterial Canvas—
A Cheek—perchance a Brow—
The Star's whole Secret—in the Lake—
Eyes were not meant to know.

CHAPTER 3

JUKE JOINTS AND TROUBLE

"Mr. Kuhner, we need you to gather your things and come with us now, please. The company helicopter is waiting and we need to take you home." It was 1946 and my father, nineteen years old, was in a small town in Texas on a summer job. But he was learning much more than the workings of an established company.

My dad loved to play the trumpet. In Hamilton College not only was his playing legendary, but he was also the leader of two bands—one for college-only functions and the other for out-of-town gigs. He could feel music down to his toes, he would tell me later. He came of age during the big-band era, but his real love was jazz. Problem was, he had little access to innovative styles in his restricted environment. My grandfather, Max Kuhner, had worked his way up to vice president of his engineering firm in Massachusetts. As a German immigrant with a thick accent, this was especially difficult in the America of the 1920s and 1930s. He did this by being extremely talented, but also by following the rules exactly. He was keenly aware of what the social and professional norms of the time were, and he followed them. His American-born son, my father, was not so constrained.

And so it was that while on that summer job in Texas (working for his father's company in a non-technical job), Fred Kuhner found himself on the company's helicopter headed back to his home in Worcester, Massachusetts, in what he was supposed to feel was disgrace. His crime? He wandered around the back roads of small Texas towns and fell into juke joints—generally all-black jazz clubs—where the music he heard "soared and then plummeted and then jumped all around the room" he told me. "It was the most interesting and emotional and inspiring stuff I had ever heard." So he took out his trumpet and joined in. "I think at first they thought I was just a curiosity, but they figured out really quickly that I loved the music as much as they did. Other parts of our lives were very different, but the real parts, the parts in our hearts and souls—the parts where music comes from—well, we were the same." Pretty soon this skinny white boy became known in those parts. "My biggest compliment was when they started calling me 'Gabriel' and they would yell out, 'Blow that horn, man! Blow down those walls!'"

Somehow, my dad's excursions got back to the managers at his father's company, and they sent a helicopter to bring him back. "It didn't look good," they told him, "being around 'those people.' It's just not right," he was told. So, he was forced to come back. His father was not happy. His friends didn't understand why he would do what he did. And no one understood when after college graduation, tired of the strings in his life, he left the plush world of his upbringing for the adventure of South America where he would meet my mother.

"Sylvia," he would tell me years later, "you've got to see people for who they are—for what they bring to the world—not what someone else decides you should think about them. We all have music inside. Listen to your own. Listen to others. Respect and enjoy it. All of life is a symphony of souls sending their songs out to the whole universe. Together the sound is magnificent."

HAMILT○NEWS

MAY 3, 1947

FRED KUHNER
CONCERTS, CARISSIMA, AND CLOSE-ORDER DRILL

CHAPTER 4

BABY BROTHER

"I guess it wasn't too unusual for an only child, but still it bordered on obsession."

From the time I could talk I would ask my mother for a baby brother. In the early 1950s in Montevideo, Uruguay, one of the ways to deflect discussions about where babies come from was to tell young kids that mail-order-like, babies come "from Paris." So, I would ask if my baby brother had come from Paris yet. I was really insistent about this point.

"What about a baby sister?" people would ask. "No, a brother," I would demand.

A few years after my mother was divorced from my biological father, who had deserted us when I was an infant, she married Fred Kuhner, who I immediately called my real father. We moved to a house in an area called Carrasco, Uruguay, and at age four I started school. Senora Gonzales was a particularly beloved teacher. While the other kids took naps on floor mats, I helped her sort materials. If anyone awoke upset or fearful I would run to their side to talk to them and make them feel better.

Nap time was my favorite part of the day. Sometimes during that part of the day I would be allowed to wander down the hall to the school library. That's where I saw it—evidence that my parents were totally ignorant about conception and birth.

"Senora Gonzales! Look, look what I found!" I called to her in as controlled a whisper-yell as my young mouth could produce. "You need to tell me the absolute truth. Do babies really come from Paris?" Well, dear readers, she felt she had no choice. The book detailed a lot, and she knew I was desperate for facts. So she explained, in what I imagine must have been rather ambiguous terms, how pregnancy happens. Apparently I was not shocked about the process—but I was shocked at my parents' lack of information.

"She called us from the school before you came home. She warned us about what had happened," my mother told me years later. "You came in the house, threw down your sweater, and demanded that your father and I sit down in the living room the instant he came home. Then you went to your room and slammed the door shut. Slammed it. I couldn't imagine what was next. I called your father to warn him and we decided what our approach would be with this situation. But I underestimated you." She sighed. She always sighed when she told this story and always emphasized how she

underestimated me. I'd heard it many, many times throughout my life, but the last time she told it was in 2001, three
years before she died. Then it became different.

But now she continued the often-told story, "When your
father came home and we settled ourselves on the sofa, I
called to you that we were ready. You came out of the bedroom with a book, some paper, and some pencils. There was
barely controlled anger and disappointment in your face. You
were always such a sunny child that this took us by surprise.
And then, putting the writing materials in front of us, you
began your lesson. 'Babies do not come from Paris. You have
been doing things all wrong. You have wasted letter after
letter sending for a baby. Let me show you what needs to happen.' And then you began drawing and explaining." At this
point she always stopped because embarrassed laughter would
overtake her and anyone else listening. She then continued,
"You asked us if we had any questions. When we shook our
heads with a 'no,' you said you expected that this knowledge
would lead to a baby brother, and you pivoted and marched
resolutely back to your room."

When my own daughter was three years old, in 1981,
my mother was visiting us during a particularly cold day in
February, and she once again over tea and cake told the story.
I then asked a question that had not occurred to me before.
"Mom, when did I give up this quest for a brother? I must
have given up at some point."

"Well," she began, "it was really very strange. For most
birthdays or holidays when asked what you wished for, you'd

say a baby brother. But several days before you turned six, you asked for something else. It was odd. 'You don't want a baby brother anymore?' I asked you. And you answered in the strangest, most eerie way, 'No, I don't need to ask anymore because he's already born.' So strange, Sylvia. So strange. But then, children say such strange things." My mother and I laughed about this as we sipped some tea and watched my daughter, her granddaughter, play with dolls.

Twenty years later, to the day (pre-internet, pre-social media, pre-easy international communications), my half-brother who—completely unbeknownst to me—searched for me most of his life, contacted me. He was currently living with his wife and three young children in Montevideo, Uruguay, where he was born on January 21 in 1956—one week before my 6th birthday.

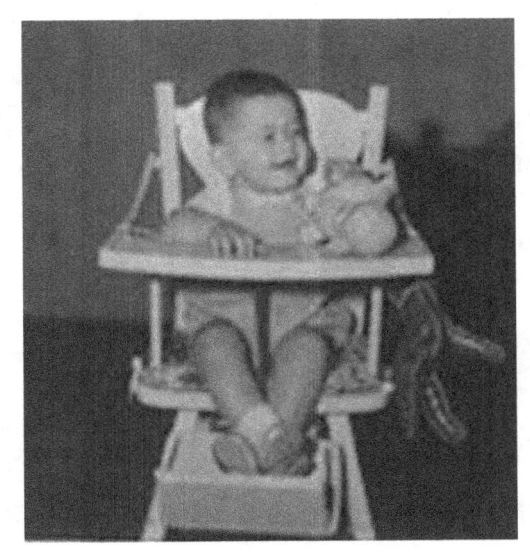

CHAPTER 5

MARIA

"Everything changed after your best friend Maria died," my mother said.

In 1976 my grandmother, my mother, and I were looking at old picture albums. When we came across a photo of me when I was five in Montevideo, Uruguay, in 1955, both stopped to reminisce. My mother continued: "It was a bright day in October, and I remember that the school called to tell me all the students had to go home.

"Polio.

"Polio had taken hold and several students were diagnosed. I picked you up, sure that everything must have been a mistake. The next day Maria died, and I thought I would lose my mind. They told us it was a virus and there was nothing to be done except keep you away from all other children. No children could play with others. And we needed to monitor you for symptoms. I was so afraid and no one seemed to understand what to do. I just looked at you—at your happy little face—and worried and fretted."

My grandmother chimed in: "As soon as I heard the panic in your mother's voice on the phone, I came right away. We were all of us at your house for weeks. Each day we would hear of a new tragedy." I remembered some of this vaguely but had never really heard them recount it so vividly. "You had a favorite dress that was too small, but you always wanted to still wear it. I would never let you do it. But during that time I told you you could put on whatever you wanted. You were so delighted and wanted us to take your photo. Here it is."

My mother pointed to me smiling in a very short pink pinafore dress. "How did you manage that stress? The fear? The isolation?" I asked them both.

My mother turned to my grandmother and (uncharacteristically) let her speak: "I reminded your mother that in 1928—we were still in Poland then—she had typhus. She was five years old. Others were dying and no one knew from where this virus came. All we could do was stay home. Isolated. Your mother was terribly sick and I was terrified. My mother-in-law came to help. And there we were alone for weeks—separated from the rest of the world, nursing your mother back to health and trying not to get the virus ourselves. Everyone in the town was quarantined. No one came out of their houses for more than simple groceries. Very little was left in stores, but it was enough. Eventually, she got better, they discovered where it came from, and we all slowly began life outside the house."

I was astonished that the two of them had such similar experiences of virus attacks and isolation. Then my mother spoke: "It was terrifying, yes, but we learned something important." My grandmother nodded as my mother continued, "We learned that at times like those there is still life. At first we did nothing but wait and watch, but then we realized that we had life and the important thing was to have it, not to lose it by fear."

Now my grandmother continued: "My mother-in-law told me that the biggest sin we could commit was to act dead when we were still alive. She would sing raucous country songs and we would laugh and dance. We drank a lot of tea and she would tell me stories of the old days. I found out that life doesn't stop because you are forced inside."

Then my mother continued, "We were so lucky that you did not get sick. After a few weeks we ventured out again and you began playing with other kids. Slowly my fear subsided. But when I look at your picture, I don't remember that time as lost—I remember that I learned more about how to live."

Yes: No matter what the circumstances, the only time that is lost—that is truly lost—as my great-grandmother, grandmother, and mother taught me, is the time you forget to live.

EMILY DICKINSON: 501

This World is not Conclusion.
A Species stands beyond—
Invisible, as Music—
But positive, as Sound—
It beckons, and it baffles—
Philosophy—don't know—
And through a Riddle, at the last—
Sagacity, must go—
To guess it, puzzles scholars—
To gain it, Men have borne
Contempt of Generations
And Crucifixion, shown—
Faith slips—and laughs, and rallies—
Blushes, if any see—
Plucks at a twig of Evidence—
And asks a Vane, the way—
Much Gesture, from the Pulpit—
Strong Hallelujahs roll—
Narcotics cannot still the Tooth
That nibbles at the soul—

CHAPTER 6

HE DIED EARLY
THIS MORNING

"He died early this morning." It was 1956, I was six years old and playing in my front yard in Montevideo, Uruguay, when she brought me the news about Coco, their dog. Susana Brusca was a close friend of my mother's, and I adored her. Two years earlier my parents had taken a four-month holiday on a luxury cruise ship, and I was left in the very capable hands of Susana and her husband. I treasured my time with them and with their dog. They were fun and happy people and I was very comfortable with them—but, unlike my family, they were very religious. Their Catholicism wasn't separate from the rest of their lives—it was their lives. During my stay they worried so much about my soul that eventually I had an "emergency baptism" administered by their priest.

In general, matters of religion were not part of my family's life. My mother's Jewish heritage and my father's Lutheran one were not routinely discussed. So when Coco died and I was despondent, Susana tried to comfort me with explanations of an afterlife and resurrection and Jesus's love for creatures of all kinds. "He will go to heaven and live with our Lord and Savior," she proclaimed with confidence. I had no real understanding of Jesus, but what I had heard about him I liked. As I saw in paintings hanging on the Bruscas' walls, he seemed to be a kind and gentle soul with sad, compassionate eyes.

"But I want Coco here with me now. Why can't he still live here?" I pleaded.

Susana explained: "Life doesn't work that way. All things that live will one day die and then they go to heaven."

This concept left me dumbfounded. I went inside to my room to think. I asked questions of my parents later, but their vague answers ("Don't worry about it—everything will be fine," "You will understand when you're older") did not satisfy my quest for enlightenment.

Two days later while visiting my grandparents I brought up the question of death—I could always count on them for truth. "Abuelo, does everything that's living die? I mean everything and everyone?" He took my small hand in his large, calloused one and led me outside. We sat on benches looking out at a muddy, small lake and he began. "Yes, Sylvia. That is true. One of the greatest things that can happen is to be born and have life. But life is limited. It has a beginning and it has an end." I sighed, understanding that he was giving me the real information here.

I continued with my question: "So what happens when we die? The Bruscas think we go to heaven, the Jewish religion doesn't really have a heaven, and I'm not sure what else there is. Do we just disappear?"

He was still holding my hand as we sat in the soft afternoon sunlight—gentle breezes blowing around us—and at this point he squeezed it tightly. He let out a sigh and continued: "I know that many religions differ about what happens after we die. But this is what I believe—all of life is connected. Every atom that ever was is right here right now. Flowers grow from soil rich in the nutrients of long-dead plants. All of life is a circle so that even though we die we still are part of the cycle of the universe. You know that fish I caught for us and we ate for lunch?" I nodded, remembering the delicious flavor of the fried fish with lemon. He continued, "Well, that fish is now part of you. It gives you nutrients that help you grow. So it's part of you, but you are also part of the fish. It lives in you. And the potatoes your grandmother cooked with delicious cheese sauce—those too are part of you and you are part of them. Everything is connected."

I could begin to see this. It was making some sense to me. But I needed more. "So, Abuelo, what happens when a person dies, or . . ." now I looked down, holding back tears "a dog?"

He smiled at me, "I think that because we are also made of matter, when we die our molecules and atoms blend with the universe. They become part of it. All of it connects. So the essence of that tiny drop of water on the edge of that leaf right there—it could have atoms from someone from thousands of years ago."

I nodded in some understanding. And then, right before standing up and heading back to the house, he looked straight at me seriously and continued, "Someday I will die. When you see a beautiful cloud think that it is a part of me. When you see leaves waving to you as you walk by, think that they are a part of me. Dogs, babies, birds—they are all part of me. And when you see someone who needs help or someone who is sad or someone who is dancing with joy—they too are part of me." He hugged me. We stood up and headed back hand in hand—a tall, slightly stooped-over, old man and a small little girl.

A few months later he died.

But here, today, now in the twenty-first century—see them?—are some palm fronds and a beautiful blue sky. They are part of him and of me and of us all.

CHAPTER 7

LO ODIO

"Lo odio!" I said of a boy who lived down the road from me in Montevideo, Uruguay. I was six years old and spending the weekend with my grandparents. My language was Spanish. Their Spanish was learned sixteen years earlier when they desperately fled to this tiny South American country from Prague, Czechoslovakia, as the Nazis were invading.

"Ah, Sylvia, no. You can be angry and upset, but 'hate' is not a word we use in any language," my grandfather admonished me. My grandmother's command of Spanish was not as strong, so she asked him to translate. "Sie hasst ihn," he said, and I saw her face grow solemn, her bright blue eyes cloud over, and her finger wag back and forth metronome-like, while saying "no, no, no."

"But he's mean," I began in Spanish, "and he always laughs at how I run, so I hate him."

We were having lunch in their small rustic home, and as my grandmother ladled steaming chicken noodle soup into simple white bowls and placed them before us on the wooden table, my grandfather began the story that I would only later in life fully understand. "You know in Prague we had a fine house. So many rooms! And tapestries on the walls and the best porcelain china in beautiful hand-painted designs. Every New Year's Eve we had a grand party with so many people all dressed in fine clothing and glittering jewelry. We built one of the first swimming pools in the country and in summers had lovely events there. When our friends began to warn us of the Nazi invasion, we didn't believe it could happen. Very quickly so many of our Jewish friends left the country, but we stayed."

Then I interrupted, "Were all of your friends Jewish like you? Were some of them Nazis?"

"Well," he continued, "it happens that some believed in the Nazi movement and some were Nazis because they were afraid not to be. We tried to not talk about it very much. We had been friends for so long that it seemed crazy to us that they would do anything terrible to us. But then we began to see the truth of our situation: If we did not leave, we would be killed." I gulped down my soup, intent on every word. He continued, "We could hear 'die Juden toten' ('kill the Jews') chanted in the streets. What filled their hearts was like a disease—a cancer—that was eating people from inside their souls—killing the humanity within them."

"It was 'odio' wasn't it, Abuelo? 'Odio.'"

"Yes, it was. It was 'hate.'" He looked at me with his almost violet blue eyes and continued, "You're old enough now, Sylvia, to know this story. Our story. And you're old enough to know that we do not say that word in any language because that word is a destroyer of the human spirit. It tries to destroy all love. But, here's the secret," he said leaning closer to me, "it can't. Yes, it can hurt and kill lots of things, but love wins. Always. It does not die."

"How did you leave?" I asked. "Friends helped us," he said.

"Oh. I thought your Jewish friends were all gone by then," I continued, thinking maybe I had gotten the story wrong.

"No," he said. "Some of our friends who were with the Nazi party knew of the invasion and they secretly helped us escape at night. See? Hate did not win the whole of their hearts. We could take very little. It was very hard for us, starting a new life, but we had our little family and we made it happy for ourselves. They took our things, but we had our love. And you see, we do not say that word because we don't want it to exist in our world. Words come out of your mouth like birds and take flight in the air and you don't know how far they travel. We do not want to send 'hate' in any form into the world."

Many years later, after my parents and I moved to the United States, after my grandparents died, after a lifetime of living, I have come to fully understand what they meant. I have come to understand the strength of people to see beyond current situations, horrific though they be, and to transcend all hatred. There is humanity in all of us. I have come to understand fully my grandfather's final statements on that day, "Words have tremendous power, Sylvia. Learn to use them well. Learn to use them in many languages so you can have understanding with many others. Words have life and must be used carefully. And then when you learn, teach others."

CHAPTER 8

CARLOTA

"Today's the big day, everyone," my grandmother said in Spanish. "Everything will be perfect. Today is for Carlota!"

We all knew her as poor Señora Carlota, who seldom left her house and whose kids were always very shy and reluctant to play with the rest of us. It was 1957, I was seven years old, and spending one of my last days in Montevideo, Uruguay, with my grandmother before my parents and I moved to the United States. Abuela's small millinery shop, La Casa de Margot, was always humming with activity, but on this afternoon it was especially busy. I watched the whirl of it all from my favorite chair by the sales counter. In the center of the store Carlota was encircled by women fixing her hair, adjusting a strap on her dress, adorning her with costume jewelry, and sizing her shoes. I could barely see her, but when I finally did, it seemed like a miracle. Señora Carlota looked radiantly beautiful.

"Jorge, the car—right now," Abuela barked at our neighbor, and he dutifully ran off to pull the old black car, which doubled as a hearse, up to the front of the store. Regally Carlota entered the car, her shiny earrings glistening—a long black-lace shawl carefully arranged to cover her bruises. Later, after everyone cleaned up the store and went home, Abuela explained things to me.

"You are old enough to know some things that happen. It's not a secret. Her husband is terrible to her," she started. "When he gets angry, he hits her." Yes, I had heard her screams from almost a block away. "With five children to take care of, she can't leave. He has control of the children and will take them away," she continued. "He calls her ugly and disgusting, and refuses to take her anywhere."

So she stayed home when she wasn't working in the shop, and late into the night, after taking care of the household's needs, she created beautiful things. Carlotta could sew and her embroidery was legendary. Birds of all colors seemed to almost rise from the linen. Intertwined circles of roses twined over pillowcases. On her children's clothes, flowers and butterflies covered the ripped parts of old dresses and pants handed down two, three, four times. The colors were so bold, so bright, they danced on the cloth.

Even with much prodding and coaxing, she would not enter her work in the yearly local festival contest. "He would be angry." Or "It's not really very good," were her reasons—her mantra. But this year, in secret, some of her friends entered a few items. When they came to tell her she'd won first prize, she clapped her hands with joy. They told everyone later that her body shook with held-back excitement as she covered her partly toothless smile with her hands.

The gift was going to be awarded at the local community center dinner the next evening, but her husband said she was too ugly to claim it. When Carlota told my grandmother about this early in the day, Abuela was determined that her friend would go. So Abuela called on many of her own friends to come and help her with clothes and hair and shoes and a car, and to take care of the children. She made Carlota a special hat, red, with a large feather that seemed to stab the air around it. And, in Jorge's sometimes-hearse, they sent her off to the event.

Years later, in 1975, Abuela was staying with me in my house in Maryland, and as she and I sat sewing one afternoon, I remembered this incident. "What ever happened to Carlota?" I asked her. Abuela laughed. "Everyone talked about it for days! When she walked into the community center her husband was so surprised to see her that he dropped his dinner plate, and it shattered loudly. The woman he was with—oh, he had a lot of mistresses—fell trying to clean up his mess. The room erupted with laughter.

"When Carlota was given the award, for the first time in her life she spoke in public, and loudly. She told everyone that she had many friends and now she knew they would always take care of her. And that she came in a hearse and would leave in a hearse, and she was no longer afraid of anyone. And as she said this, she looked at her husband straight in the eyes."

Abuela laughed again. "Oh, I wish I had been there! It was legendary. Three days later her husband died of a heart attack. He was in bed with one of his mistresses. The next year Carlota married Jorge. Can you believe it? Jorge!" Abuela shook her head and giggled. "And he always called her his 'princess.' They still live in Montevideo. In a big house now. His funeral business took off, and she became very famous for creating embroideries and laces for expensive clothes."

"Why didn't you go to the event?" I asked her—a question I had not considered before. She looked up from her sewing and smiled: "Because you were leaving in two days for such a faraway place—a whole new country—and I knew I wouldn't see you for a long time. And before you left I wanted you to see—I wanted to tell you—that no matter what happens to you, no matter how bad a situation might be, there are always good people ready to help you."

She was right.

CHAPTER 9

GRANDMOTHER'S PERFUME

"It's time for a new adventure!" my grandfather called out as he handed me a strange white outfit with a sort of mesh headpiece. It was summer 1956, I was almost seven years old and staying with my grandparents for a few days. I loved their little country house and spent endless hours with both of them exploring the surrounding area. Down the long dirt lane there was a muddy pond and just a little further on a field of tall grasses where I'd squat down to watch crawling bugs and find a stray feather or two to examine with my trusty magnifying glass. When I'd rush back into the house carting rocks or empty snail shells or bits of colorful flowers one or the other of my grandparents would eagerly make space on the weathered oak kitchen table to delight in my treasures. "The world is full of marvels, Sylvia, and it's all connected. Down to even the tiniest drop of water—all of the natural things in the whole world are connected in ways that we can just begin to understand," they'd tell me.

They knew, but I didn't grasp, that in a few weeks I would be moving from Uruguay, where I was born and where they now lived, to the United States—my new father's country. They knew this was going to be my last visit to their cottage.

On this particular day I had spent a longer time than usual watching my grandmother's morning ritual of combing her white hair and securing it atop her head, using a large puff to lightly powder her face, and dabbing an exotic-scented perfume behind her ears and on her wrists. As always, she inhaled it deeply—eyes closed—and smile. "Divino" she'd say in Spanish, "divine." The scent would linger in the house for hours and even later in the day, returning from one of my many adventures, I would still catch it wafting in the air.

"This is a special protective suit," Abuelo began as he burst into the room, "and we're going to see Jose Alvarez's beehives close-up." I jumped up and down, unable to contain my excitement. For several summers I had heard the murmuring buzz of the nearby apiary and had tasted the delicious honey, but I was too young, Jose Alvarez stated unequivocally, to get close up. But now—now I was ready. My grandfather and I put on our outfits, pulled on the headgear, and awkwardly trudged toward the bees.

In words that a young child could understand, Jose Alvarez explained the workings of the hive. I was stunned and elated by all of it and excitedly related my new knowledge to my grandmother a few hours later over tea and honey-laced biscuits. I began, "Did you know that bees can smell? And that they have special dances that they use to sort of talk? And that each one has a special job they do so that the whole hive will work—so that they have to cooperate to make things better for everyone?"

Now my grandfather jumped in, "And do they always stay in the same place? Do they stay in the same hive?"

"No," I answered putting down my cookie and spreading my arms out for emphasis. "When the bees in charge decide it's time for a change—there are lots of reasons for this—they move to find a different place to live." I looked over at my grandmother, but she had gotten up and was now bent over the sink, her back to me. My grandfather, seeing her, quickly got up from his chair and stood next to her—his arm wrapping around her shoulders.

I left for the United States two weeks later. They died two years later. I never saw my grandparents again.

In 1987, to celebrate my newly earned PhD, one of my mother's very stylish friends brought me an elaborately wrapped present that a saleswoman had recommended. As I opened it my mom and I both gasped—there it was—the same perfume my grandmother used, Guerlain's Mitsouku. I opened the bottle and she was right there in the room with us, floating around and above and through our celebration.

I was in tears as my mother began, "You know, your grandmother told me the story: She couldn't bring much with her when they escaped from Prague right before the war. And there was so much pain and misery in their early, lean years in Uruguay. Then their son, your biological father, turned out to be such a scoundrel and a danger to everyone. But on the day you were born, your grandfather bought a bottle of this perfume, your grandmother's favorite from their early, happy years when they lived in Europe, and gave it to her. She told me that the smell reminded her of beginnings. She told me this the day before we left for our new home." I had never heard this before. Now my mother continued, "When you embraced her for a final good-bye before leaving for our new country you seemed to cling to her a long time, breathing deeply. And your grandfather . . ." now my mother's voice was shaky and long forgotten tears filled her eyes, "he looked at you and said, 'Remember, starting a new hive is a wonderful adventure.' I didn't know what that meant but on our long plane ride, you explained."

And today, as I find myself even older than my grandparents were the last time I saw them, my eleven-year-old grandson cut some lavender from my garden which he's been helping me tend and handed it to me after burying his nose and taking a big whiff. He smiled and said, "When I smell lavender, it always makes me think of you."

CHAPTER 10

MY GIFT TO YOU

"Why did they do that? I don't understand," I said in Spanish, the only language I knew at the time, and the one my grandparents had needed to quickly learn. It was 1956, I was six years old, and while my grandmother cooked dinner, my grandfather Meindl and I sat at the big wooden table in their dining room in Montevideo. I had been going to their house for dinner almost every Sunday night of my life. After dinner he would sometimes read me stories or write me poems. On this particular night I became fascinated with some small paintings he had made that I found on the side-board. "These are all birds, Abuelo. I didn't know you liked birds. They're beautiful."

He looked at them carefully, one by one, and for the first time in my life I saw his eyes fill up with tears. "Why are you sad?" I asked, very confused, and continued, "They're really pretty."

He set them down on the table and sat me down on the chair facing him. "I think you're old enough to know this," he began. Then he continued, "You know that we lived in Prague. We had such a beautiful house there. We had fine porcelains and art and lovely gardens full of flowers that your grandmother tended and adored. For me, the most glorious part of the whole house was a library I designed and filled with book after book after book. I had some of the best and most interesting minds right there on my shelves always ready to entertain or teach or help me."

Now he stopped and asked me, "You understand what I mean by that, don't you, Sylvia?" I nodded enthusiastically, remembering my love of going to the library and picking out my very own books. "Well," he continued, "I had to leave all of those behind when we were forced to leave our home and a lot of our family. The Nazis were coming and we had help getting out of the country, but we had to leave so much behind. Some of our friends said they would try to send things to us later. And they did send some . . ." Now his voice trailed off and he looked back at his paintings and with a deep sigh continued, "but no books. They could not send any books."

Now my grandmother came into the room from the kitchen, wiping her hands on her ruffled blue-and-white apron and spoke quickly to my abuelo. It was a heated exchange in the Czech language that I did not understand. But I could hear the anger and saw her pointing to me and my grandfather answering forcefully. Then she bent her white-gray head level with mine. Her blue eyes blazing, she hugged me and left the room.

"Your grandmother doesn't think you should hear such things, but I think you're old enough to know a little of what happened to us. We are your history. You need to know history to try to make the future better." He stopped for a moment and then continued. "We never thought they would do what they did. Germany was always the place of high intellect and art and music. Such a beautiful country. And such civilization and culture! Ah. We could almost not believe it when the German Nazis started burning the books. Burning books! It made no sense to any of us."

I was stunned and interrupted, "Why would anyone want to do that, Abuelo? Why?" He looked at me and continued, "That, I don't really know. Fear I think. When people are afraid they do strange things. And sometimes that fear makes them want to get rid of what they imagine is attacking them."

"But, books can't attack anyone," I responded. Now I was getting upset. He continued, "What people fear from books are ideas. And the Nazis thought that if they burned the books and . . ." he stopped himself, then continued, "tried to get rid of people they were afraid of, then those ideas would go away."

I laughed. "Abuelo, ideas don't go away. They're right here," I said pointing to my head.

He smiled and continued, "Right you are, my little one. Right you are. But there was a war and they invaded Prague and we had to leave our old country for this new country, so you could be born."

Now he hugged me and I giggled and as my grandmother brought in our delicious, steaming hot soup, I asked him, "But why didn't you get your books after the war?" Stirring the heat out of my bowl and moving the wide, handmade noodles through the broth, he continued.

"You see, when they invaded our city, they came to our house and . . . and . . . and they burned all of my books. Took them down from the shelves and tossed them in a big flame in the garden. In the middle of your grandmother's garden. We were told people could see the tall flames from blocks away."

I was horrified but he continued, "We were here in this wonderful country when I heard of that. And I decided that maybe they could burn my books and all the books in the world if they wanted to, but they could not burn my soul, they could not burn my memories, they could not burn my heart.

"So I started painting birds that I remembered that came to your grandmother's garden. Birds can fly and they're beautiful—just like our minds. See, this one is a datel (a wood-pecker), this one a hyl (bullfinch), this is a lednack (kingfisher)."

"And what is that one? I think that's my favorite," I stated. He smiled, "Oh, my granddaughter, that one is the mir bird—the rarest of birds in the world. My wish is that you will someday find him." Now my grandmother smiled broadly. Both of them repeated the name several times—chant-like: mir, mir, mir.

"Can I keep this?" I pleaded. He nodded an enthusiastic yes. Then I put my small hand on his wool-sweatered arm, looked up at him in complete earnestness and said, "One day, Abuelo, I will build you a new library. And I will fill it full, full, full of books! And I'll hang this up on the wall." He laughed with delight and we all dipped our spoons into the nourishing soup.

It was not until just recently, decades after that day, that I learned the truth about my favorite bird—the one my grandfather gave me to carry into the future. The one that now hangs in my home's newly built, book-filled library. There is no such bird in nature.

"Mir" is the word in Czech for "peace."

CHAPTER 11

TWIGS

In February 1939, a month before the Nazi invasion, my grandparents had to flee from their home and family in Prague. My grandfather was Jewish, and they knew what was going to happen. They hastily gathered what they could carry and left the rest to the care of neighbors and of fate.

They settled in the small country of Uruguay, in South America. Decades later, when I was a child and lived near them, I'd visit their tiny plot of land in the countryside and revel in delight when it was grape season. The purple plump juiciness would dribble down my chin as I ate handfuls of them.

One day when I was almost seven Abuelo told me, "When we had to leave Czechoslovakia there was not much we could take, but I took a shriveled-up piece of a grape vine. I knew

I could root it and make a new arbor wherever we ended up. It looked like death, but I knew it was hope. You see, Sylvia, through the rest of life you always have to carry the possibility for growth with you. Always have it in your pocket, in your heart, and in your soul. Even withered-looking twigs can grow with the right soil and air and care."

A month later my parents and I moved to the U.S., and I never saw my grandparents again. But I always carry the reminder of the twig of growth and hope inside my soul.

Emily Dickinson: 326

I cannot dance upon my Toes—
No Man instructed me—
But oftentimes, among my mind
A Glee possesseth me

That had I Ballet—knowledge—
Would put itself abroad
In Pirouette to blanch a Troupe—
Or lay a Prima—mad—

And though I had no Gown of Gauze—
No Ringlet, to my Hair—
Nor hopped to Audiences—like Birds—
One Claw upon the Air—

Nor tossed my shape in Eider Balls—
Nor rolled on Wheels of Snow
Till I was out of sight in sound—
The House encore me so—

Nor any know I know the Art
I mention—easy—Here—
Nor any Placard boast me—
It's full as Opera—

CHAPTER 12

JELLY

In 1957, the day after we landed in Dallas after a twenty-four-hour, two-stop airplane (no jets yet) journey from Montevideo, Uruguay, we began another trip. This time we crossed the country by car—first to California and then across the great continent that I immediately loved.

I was seven, and our finances and spaces were very limited so I had no toys. None. The first morning though, brought me a new wonder—with my toast came small aluminum jelly containers (now they're plastic). After emptying two of them and washing them out in the bathroom, I started creating things with them while my parents finished their coffee. They became tiny boats for imaginary tiny people. And when those people got tired, they became tiny beds. A waitress helped me make little sails for them by cutting up some napkins. So began my trek across the country.

I remember a great deal about that two-month trip, but warmest of all are my memories of waitresses. In each restaurant I entered with my ever-increasing collection of containers, one or two waitresses would contribute something to my stash. I still couldn't speak English, but my American father would explain that these were my only toys as I spread them out on the table in front of me and began my adventures. One waitress showed me how to make little people out of toothpicks; another made me tiny bananas from Juicy Fruit gum wrappers; another one cut a tiny picture of a tree out of a magazine so they could have shade. And so it went. All across the country—Nevada, Oklahoma, Arkansas, Minnesota, and points east, waitresses helped my collection and my imagination.

Years later while wading through my daughter's toy room, my father and I reflected on my childhood and our adventures. I reminisced about the wonderful waitresses who helped me create my tiny container worlds and how caring they were. "It's funny," he remarked, "what I remember is how happy you made them. Some of those stops were run-down and seedy, but you never saw that. You were just happy and thankful. You made those women smile at your little towns and for just a few minutes they had some fun. One waitress—I think it was in Arizona—had been mourning the death of her daughter for months—the manager told us this when she went back to her pocketbook to get you something for your little aluminum town. But that waitress was really happy playing with you—first time they saw her smile in a very long time."

I scanned my memory for what she could have given me. Then I found it: "Was she the one who gave me the lace hankie?" "Yes, that's it," my father continued, "she said she had cried enough and now she wanted that hankie to go on to a happier life. It was her daughter's."

I jumped in: "I remember she told me that my people might get cold, and she wanted them to have something to warm them, so we made it into a blanket."

Warmth. And so, this odyssey—this sharing of joy and grief and hope and loss and resilience was the America I found at the age of seven. It's still the one I live in today.

CHAPTER 13

ROYALTY

"Oh, she was a grand woman! Very noble." When, at seven years old, I first heard this about Ana, my great-grandmother, I envisioned gowns, and jewels, and even a flowing velvet cape. But, of course, I was very wrong. She was far greater than that.

In 1930 my Jewish grandmother Margot, with her two small children (Sara and Max) emigrated from Poland to South America. She was escaping the pain of a ruthless regime of terror and destruction. My great-grandmother, Ana, who had nursed my mother and her brother through several dangerous illnesses, was heartbroken at the thought of losing her daughter and grandchildren to another continent. But part they must. Several years later Ana died.

The 1940s brought horrors to the family in Poland with many killed in concentration and labor camps and many others simply murdered in their homes. All communication had stopped. It was not until the early 1950s that several of the remaining relatives and friends were able to emigrate, and some came to stay with us in our tiny city of Montevideo, Uruguay. I was a young child, but I loved their stories and the word-pictures they would paint of that old world they had left. I asked about my great-grandmother Ana, whom my mother had mentioned. What had happened to that grand, fine, noble woman?

"She died of a long illness," they told me. "But it was an amazing thing when she died. It was instructed that Jews were not allowed formal burials. They were just dumped into graves. But not your great-grandmother."

"Why not?" I asked. "Was she royalty?"

Gentle laughter ensued. "Yes, but maybe not in the way you imagine. It was because all her life she helped the poor. If she had one piece of bread left, she would give half of it to the poor and half to her family and she would eat nothing. If she had two pieces of cloth, she would sew a dress for a desperate child."

"So, she helped the Jewish community," I mused.

"No," I was told, "not just that community. She helped everyone who needed her help. The Catholic people of the town loved her so much that when she died, they carried her coffin to the cemetery. Even the soldiers on watch did not disturb the ceremony. No one had ever seen anything like that before. We knew, all of us, that this was the last moment we could all honor goodness in the world. She helped others because it was the right thing to do—even in the middle of evil as the armies snatched her children and grandchildren and sent them to die in camps. Even as her house and her small possessions were confiscated. She helped others. They called her 'The Queen of the Good World.'"

And then these ancients, my historians, the carriers of the past, cast their heads down with long, heavy sighs. Even as a child I felt their sighs in my bones.

I feel them still.

CHAPTER 14

FROSTY

"¿De que trata ese libro?" ("What is that book about?")
my mother asked me.

It was May 1957, I was seven years old, and my mother
and I were alone in our new home in Larchmont, New York.
We had arrived from Montevideo just a few months earlier,
and I had been busily learning the English language from
the moment we landed in Dallas. The television programs I
watched in various motel rooms as my parents and I criss-
crossed the continent while my father searched for jobs were
very helpful—I could spout the jingles before I ever understood
their meanings. ("Brylcreem, a little dab'll do you . . .") But
here in Larchmont, another temporary perch, I actually got
to go to school, and the special immigrant programs helped
my language skills immediately. Miss Kelly was my favorite
teacher; she really understood my need to learn. After only

a few months she declared me her "star pupil," and awarded me my own Golden Book one Friday afternoon, to take from her collection.

"Pick carefully," she told me, "because this will be your very first book in English. It might stay with you your whole life." Soon my delight turned grim. "What's the matter, Sylvia?" she asked. I explained that the monumental weight of that decision was very great. "Ah, what you are feeling is like despair," she said, and continued, "Despair is when you feel so terribly lost that you feel things will never be right." Yes, that was the word. I said it to myself over and over. And then my eyes saw it—the book. My book.

I took it home and eagerly read about children finding a magic hat and creating a snowman and having adventures all over town. I had never seen a snowman before, but a freakish March snowstorm had at least given me some understanding of the fluffy white stuff. And this snowman even had a name, Frosty. But then disaster struck in the form of the sun. Suddenly all of the joy was gone as the children saw their creation melt away. I started to cry as I closed the book. No amount of Frosty's theoretically comforting words about retuning next year rang true to me. I knew too much about impermanence—about loss. Right this very minute my father was off in another town looking for a job that would take us away from Larchmont. And Miss Kelly. I knew it would end again and again and again.

I couldn't bear to explain it to my already anxious mother when she asked about the story. I just said it was a silly book, and put it with my other school supplies. On Monday morning when I saw Miss Kelly she immediately asked about the book. "Here," I said, handing it to her, "I don't think I want to keep it."

She looked shocked and asked, "You love books so much. Why not this one? Did you understand it?"

"Yes," I blurted out "it's about despair. Nothing lasts, Miss Kelly. Not even snowmen."

"Ah, you used the new word well," she began with a sigh. "But I don't think that is really what is important in this story." Now I looked up at her, hopeful she could help.

"No," she continued, "the real magic in this story is in two parts. The first part is that the children all played together. What Frosty did was make them laugh and play together. They became a group of friends. It's the happiness of laughing with friends—that's the real joy. That's the real magic." This was beginning to make sense to me now. She continued, "Do you think you know what the second important thing is about the story?"

I thought really hard. I went over all of the events. I felt the emotions the children felt when introduced to magic and to song and to creating. Then I came up with the answer, "Yes! It's about making a story that reminds people that life is full of bad and good and fun and . . . and even despair." As she hugged me, I thought I saw tears in her eyes for a moment. And then she signed my book, right there on the inside cover and told me I could take it home to start my very own library.

Two weeks later we moved.

I have kept that precious book for years—from one move to another—from one country to another. As I acquired books in several languages and as my reading tastes became more and more complex, it still had pride of place on my bookshelves. It wasn't until many years later that I learned that Miss Kelly had died not too long after I left at the end of the school year. That whole time she was teaching me she was also battling cancer. She knew she was dying when she wrote the inscription in my *Frosty, The Snowman* book: "It is not the despair at loss that we should remember, but the joy— the magic—of discovering friends in even the most unlikely places. That's what stays with us, no matter where we are."

And now, I send this magic—perhaps in the midst of despair—out to all of you, my friends in even the most unlikely places.

CHAPTER 15

ETHICS

"Sylvia, you are just another stupid foreigner."

It was fall 1957, I was seven years old, and my teacher, Mrs. Barnes, said this in front of the class. I didn't understand what she was trying to say. Several months earlier, in February, I had arrived from South America not knowing any English at all and entered the second half of first grade. With a lot of practice and help I had learned enough of the language to skip the entire second-grade curriculum and land in third grade in September. I knew the "stupid" part didn't mean what I thought it meant. But she was right—I was a foreigner.

At recess I asked my best friend, Patty, to explain it to me and she said, "Well, I think she thought you didn't do the right thing in the class election today." Now, I was more confused. We were learning about voting and an exercise that we

85

did in class was to elect a class president, vice-president, trea-surer, and secretary. Each job's responsibilities were detailed by Mrs. Barnes. Then someone nominated a person for the position, that person was seconded, and their name went on the board. Two names were placed for each. I was surprised to be nominated for secretary and my name went on the board alongside Betty Granger.

I didn't know Betty very well, but I knew her to be the tidiest of all of us. Her crisp dresses were always perfectly creased, her wavy golden hair was held back perfectly with barrettes, and her classroom cubby never had awkward pieces of paper spewing out. She was dedicated to neatness and order—the opposite of me. The job of the secretary required taking care of the class plant—a big-leafed, dark green mon-ster which our teacher was very proud of. "I've been teaching for fifteen years and this plant has been taken care of perfectly all this time," she told us.

I loved seeing my name on the board and felt a touch of arrogance at my fame, but I had nagging doubts. Betty was responsible and neat. She would take much better care of the plant than I would—I knew this—I was sure of this. We voted by a show of hands and when the voting came for secretary, I lost by one vote. Mine. I voted for Betty. Mrs. Barnes contin-ued her attack, "When you are a foreigner you just don't have any sense of what is right—look at Sylvia." Everyone turned to look at me and, not understanding the situation, I smiled and waved.

After school Patty and I went over to her house where her mother was simmering a giant vat of tomato sauce with meatballs. The scent of it glided over and around me and hugged me in comfort. Patty's parents were from Italy, having arrived in this country a year before she was born. Everything they had was lost in the war and coming here meant starting over and having hope. Their dry-cleaning business had started to be profitable, and they looked forward to being able to buy a house soon. "With a room for me," Patty would exclaim, "so I won't have to sleep in the living room!"

"Mrs. Bartolli," I began as I sat at the kitchen table, "something happened at school that we don't understand. Can you explain it to us? What did I do that was stupid?" And I recounted the events of the election. As I spoke, her face got redder and redder. She yanked off her tomato-splattered apron and took me by the hand into a small alcove of the kitchen. On the wall she pointed to a photograph of an old man and woman with a small boy standing between them.

"Those were my parents and our son, Joseph," she began. "We took that picture in 1943 in a park. I asked them to pose in front of that beautiful tree. Mr. Bartolli and I walked back home and Mamma and Papa took Joseph for a candy treat. They were killed by Nazi soldiers. Killed buying a little candy. Shot. And why? Why do these things happen? It's because sometimes people just want power over others, and they forget what's right and wrong. They don't stop to think—they just grab."

I was stunned and Patty's head was bowed down. "But Sylvia, you did the right thing today. Instead of just wanting to show off you decided what the right thing was, and you did it. In English that word is 'ethical.'"

"And here is the secret," I leaned closer, "being ethical—that—that is the real power, because maybe immediately it seems to make no difference and you might get made fun of, but eventually the right way—the ethical way—always puts more good into the world." She hugged me and continued, "The more you learn about this great country that we live in, the more you will realize that everyone—everyone—has foreigners somewhere in their family. And see, it's like this big pot of sauce here, full of lots of different ingredients all bubbling away together. Delicious!"

I walked home later that afternoon and my mother was setting the table for dinner. As was her habit in Spanish she asked me, "What did you learn at school today, Sylvia?" And as was my habit I didn't tell her too many details because she simply didn't yet understand the school system or American ways. But today I told her that I learned a new word and it would be—I declared—my favorite word forever: ethical.

And it still is.

EMILY DICKINSON: 747

It dropped so low—in my Regard—
I heard it hit the Ground—
And go to pieces on the Stones
At bottom of my Mind—

Yet blamed the Fate that flung it—less
Than I denounced Myself,
For entertaining Plated Wares
Upon my Silver Shelf—

CHAPTER 16

PUNCHED IN THE FACE

When I was seven I was punched in the face for the first (and last) time in my life.

It was early September 1957. Just that February we had moved to the U.S. from Uruguay, and thanks to an amazing program in the New York public schools, I had learned enough English to not only finish first grade, but, when I moved to Passaic, New Jersey, in August, to skip into third grade.

It was recess, one warm, Monday afternoon, and I was waiting patiently in line with all the other girls to play jump rope. Two girls swung the rope, and if you were jumping and missed, you were out. I was pretty good and the line had become shorter. My starched bright white dress was starting to chafe my neck and arms a bit and to crinkle, so I patted it down.

Then, with no warning, the fifth-grade girl behind me tapped me on the shoulder. When I turned around, I felt her fist on my face. I heard her yell, "Get out of here, foreigner. We don't want you filthy people."

At first I was frozen, facing her, but suddenly I felt warmth flowing from my nose, my mouth. My dress now had red streaks down the front as I ran inside the building to the nurse. I remember kind faces from the adults, but no advice. What could they tell me, anyway?

At home I never told my mother exactly what had happened. "Jugando, playing," I said.

The next day, Tuesday, I took the one book I owned to school: *Caperucita Roja–Little Red Riding Hood.* At recess I showed some of the girls how it's the same story but in a different language. We giggled and ran around pretending to be lost in the woods.

On Wednesday one girl, Sally, brought in some pierogies her Polish grandmother made, and we discovered that three of us had Polish grandparents. And on Thursday Patty brought in some calzone her Italian mom cooked and we all shared it. Then on Friday, Carol brought a piece of bright gold cloth from her Armenian grandmother who had worn it as a scarf when she came by ship to America long ago. Giggling and happy, we took turns dancing and twirling with it held up to the blue sky.

CHAPTER 17

MAGNIFICENCE

"No. Marta Sanchez isn't coming. She wasn't invited." It was May 1958, I was eight years old and at Susie's house, three doors down from mine in Passaic, New Jersey. We were talking about an end-of-the-school-year party at her house on the coming Saturday. Susie's house was the biggest and most perfect one in town, with a pool in the backyard (with a slide!), a treehouse for her brothers that was off-limits to girls, and a permanently set-up croquet course, where we were talking.

"But she has to come. I thought everyone from our class was coming," I blurted out while banging my mallet against the wooden ball, sending it precisely through the hoop. I continued, "Her mom even made us matching dresses." Marta's mom was known to be an excellent seamstress. Her work on wedding gowns was in constant demand. She would sometimes show me how to stich around a button, or under a complicated pleat, or behind an intricate embroidered area and tell me, "It has to look like it's floating. It has to look like angels made it with magic." Then she'd smile, look at me through her thick-lensed glasses, and get back to work.

"My mom says that she's Puerto Rican and they don't belong at our parties," Susie continued as she took her turn, hit the ball, and missed the hoop. Suddenly Mrs. Tannor appeared, holding a tray of lemonade and cookies, her heavy gold charm bracelet clanging as she walked.

"Are you girls having fun?" She set things down on a nearby table, smiled and was beginning to walk away when I stopped her.

"Susie says that Marta Sanchez can't come to our party next week because she's Puerto Rican. I don't understand. She's really nice. Everyone likes her. She says she's going to be a doctor one day."

Mrs. Tannor sat down on a nearby chaise lounge, her soft yellow dress rustling around her, and motioned me to stand before her. With great solemnity she took my hands and looked me in the eyes. "Sylvia, dear, there are things in this world you just don't understand yet. There are people we simply can't be seen with. There is such a thing as a reputation and if you are with the wrong people . . . well, it's shattered. You have to be very careful in this world. And she will not be a doctor. She's a girl—and look where she comes from."

I stood frozen with my wooden mallet in my hand as she stood up quickly, patted me on my head, told us we only had a few more minutes to play, and went back to the house. "Come on, Sylvia, we've got to finish. You're beating me. You always beat me," Susie giggled.

The situation troubled me, and I thought it over and over in my mind as I trudged solemnly home. The next day at lunch I talked to Marta about this. She didn't seem surprised. "My mom says this happens to us sometimes. But she tells me not to worry because when someone doesn't like you even before they know you it's not you they don't like. It's something in themselves that they don't like but they have to find an outside place to put it. How can anyone really not like you when they don't know you? She says, 'Don't listen to hate when it talks, Marta, because it will stop you. You are made of starlight, so just shine and the whole world will see you are magnificent.'" "Magnificent" became my favorite word for the whole day.

That night at dinner I told my father about the problem. His face was red with anger, but his words were controlled and clear, "Well, you know how your mother and I feel about justice. You know how we feel that all people deserve dignity and respect and equal chances. There is a great deal of unfairness in the world. But this is becoming your world now—how do you think you should solve this?" I was confused. The party would be so much fun, but how could I enjoy it without my friend Marta there? And the matching dresses were beautiful.

I came up with a plan.

I told Susie I was really sorry, but I wouldn't be able to come to the party. I asked Marta to come to my house for an adventure on the party day and that we needed to wear our matching dresses. My mother called her mom to get her approval and when they arrived, as Marta and I twirled around in our fancy white dresses with pale blue lace trim, I saw the adults talking but couldn't hear any of the words. And then all of us climbed into my parents' big black Buick, drove over the George Washington Bridge into New York City, and on to the Plaza Hotel for afternoon tea. We ate cookies and scones and whipped cream (right off the spoon!) and cakes. Then Marta and I were allowed to wander through the lobby by ourselves. We hid behind the huge potted palms and scampered and slid on the shiny corridors. Someone stopped us and asked if we were twins and we looked at each other and burst out "*yes!*" at the same time.

On the way home we sang songs in the car and the adults told stories about when they were kids. The sun was almost setting as we drove west over the bridge on the way back to New Jersey and when we said our goodbyes, we all declared it to be "The best day ever!" I yelled loudly as they drove away, "It was magnificent!"

We moved away the following month and continued move after move for many years. As happens, I lost touch with many of my childhood friends. But by chance I ran into Susie at an event almost thirty years later. We didn't recognize each other at first but small talk about backgrounds quickly sorted that out. I asked about her family. "Well, I married a lawyer—he specializes in civil rights lawsuits. He and my mother barely talk to each other. I love her, but I just can't agree with her ideas. It took me too long," she looked down with sadness and continued, "but I did finally realize that people need to be treated with dignity. I remember listening to Martin Luther King's speech and his line about basing your opinions about folks not on the externals but on the content of the character of the individual." She went on, "My father died a few years ago. Heart attack. And my mother . . . Oh my . . ." now she chuckled at some long-held internal joke, "she had breast cancer." I looked confused, but she continued, "So her doctor sent her to the best specialist and most meticulous surgeon in New York." At this point she was laughing so hard that she wiped tears from her eyes. "I went with her for the examination and imagine both of our surprised faces when we were greeted by Marta Sanchez!" Oh my. Now I burst out laughing.

"My Marta?" I sputtered, "Marta? So, what happened next?"

"Well, she had the surgery and it was successful. Marta saved her life. And while my mom was in the recovery room and Marta came out to talk with me, I listened carefully to all instructions about after-care, thanked her, and then I asked her how she could put aside such anger and obstacles that she was faced with. And know what she told me?" Now I was listening very intently as she continued, "She said you just have to love the world. You have to make things better that you can make better. That you just have to harness your internal starshine and glow brilliantly, and eventually everyone will see your magnificence—that her mom taught her that."

CHAPTER 18

VANISH

I was horrified. "How could it just . . . vanish? That's not possible." It was 1959, I was almost nine years old, and four weeks earlier we had moved to San Paulo, Brazil—the fourth country I had lived in. My father, just thirty-one years old at the time, was starting a new enterprise: a textile factory. I had gone with him during the machinery installation and loved sitting on a high perch watching it all come together and listening to the language I was just beginning to learn—Portuguese. The men had books with instructions and suggestions for how to make it happen and slowly the design took shape. But today when I came home from school, I found my parents talking animatedly about what happened that day. My mother was waving her arms about in a state of near panic, and my father was trying to console her. "Sara," he began, "these things happen. It's not too bad. We'll fix it soon and we can get back on schedule."

There had been a small fire in the back warehouse of the factory and while some inventory had burned, the machinery was fine, he explained to me. I nodded in understanding, and, remembering the large concrete partition between the front and the back, I explained to my mother that it would be just fine. "It's not like the Library of Alexandria disaster," he said off-handedly. Confused, I asked him what that was. "It was a very ancient library that held much of the knowledge of the world. Great writers and philosophers and thinkers wrote on papyrus scrolls—what they used before our modern paper— and stacked them in this huge and beautiful library. Being a librarian there was a very prestigious position which came with a great deal of power and honor. And then almost two thousand years ago the entire library was destroyed by a giant fire. And by neglect. The whole thing was gone."

"None of it was left?" I asked in horror.

"No. Nothing. Imagine all of that information and knowledge of the world and of people gone," he explained.

I grabbed my light jacket, told my parents where I was going, and ran down the block to our local library. No matter where my parents moved us to, I always found the closest library and made it a kind of home. I loved sitting on the chairs or comfy couches, surrounded by hundreds of books, and leafing quietly through one or two or three. Sometimes I would walk around the stacks and just run my hands along the books' spines and then let my fingers feel the embossed titles on the sides or the fronts of the covers. My problem came with the language. I had learned my first language, Spanish, in Uruguay, and then learned my next language, English, when I was seven and we moved to my father's home country, the United States.

But now Portuguese was a new challenge. The library clerks were at first surprised to see an eight-year-old who couldn't speak their language showing up several afternoons a week. They would smile at me welcomingly as I bounced recklessly up and down the aisles. But no matter how hard I tried, I could not yet read any of the books.

"No English?" I would ask.

"No . . ." they would respond sadly. But I was not deterred. Every Monday, Wednesday, and Friday I would still show up.

We started learning each other's language. "Book," I would say, pointing.

"Livro," they would respond, smiling.

"Pencil," I would say; "lapis," they would answer. And so it went for several weeks. They would sometimes have picture books or art books for me to peruse when I came in. But just walking around in the midst of all of those words between covers waiting for me to discover their secrets was enough of a joy for me.

On this day, though, I needed to share this horrific new knowledge about the burnt library. I burst into the San Paulo library and kept repeating that the Alexandria library burned. "Tragedy—tragedia—Alexandria biblioteca," I blurted breathlessly as I ran into the marble building with socks slithering down my skinny legs, jacket half off my arms, hair tumbling out of my normally tight braids. They looked confused and dismayed. The head librarian came out from the back room, and I repeated the words to her.

"Ah, si," she said, shaking her head and sighing an expiration I myself could feel. "Tragedia. Grande tragedia." And then in Portuguese I could see and hear her explaining to the women about the ancient library and its demise. I didn't understand most of the words, but I could read the women's faces clearly.

"Tudo?" (everything) one of them uttered in disbelief.

"Tudo," explained the head librarian. And they looked at me, a disheveled eight-year-old girl whose place of happiness and comfort was where they worked day in and day out; a little girl who could not yet read the words in this world of theirs but somehow understood their power; a little girl standing before them feeling her first encounter with the immensity of loss—and they all reached down to hug me. One by one, with tears in their eyes, they hugged me. And for that moment, on a Wednesday afternoon, in San Paulo, Brazil, no words were necessary.

Within a month the textile factory was running smoothly. I would visit with my dad and see the weaving of the lined-up threads somehow magically finding their ways through metal to come out changed into cloth. One time I took samples of the various woven fabrics, and over the weekend made bookmarks for my librarian friends which I stored carefully in my pockets. But when I walked into the library that

Monday afternoon, they were lined up waiting for me and giggling with anticipation. I was confused. Then three of them pulled out books they were hiding behind their backs. One excitedly said, "We buy books for biblioteca—library." And they handed me three books in English. The books were about Abraham Lincoln, George Washington, and Thomas Jefferson. I jumped up and down.

"I can read these. I can read these," I chanted with glee. "Thank you!" And immediately I plunked myself down on the nearest couch and read. When I looked up, I could see them beaming. Before I left I remembered to give them the bookmarks I had made which they delightedly accepted, commenting admiringly about the different patterns and colors.

Every time I went to the library for the rest of the year they ceremoniously and with great joy brought me those three books. And even if I didn't re-read them each time, I carried them about proudly as I wandered—and sometimes skipped— down the aisles.

When I was almost ten we moved away from Brazil and back to the United States. The day before we left I said good-bye to my librarian friends. "Nos sentiremos sua falta," they said in unison.

I smiled, "I will miss you too," I answered hugging each of them. One of women solemnly continued: "Alexandria not gone," she said, "it here always," and she pointed to her heart and her head, and then to my heart and my head. And as I walked out through the large wooden door, they waved goodbye using the multi-colored woven bookmarks I had given them like signal flags on passing ships.

Many years later I learned that the government in Brazil during that time had no money for library books in foreign languages. And that these women, who had to commute several hours a day to their jobs for very low pay, lived in small homes in the back country with little running water and electricity. And I learned that for months they had saved small amounts every week so that they themselves could buy those books so that I could read in their library.

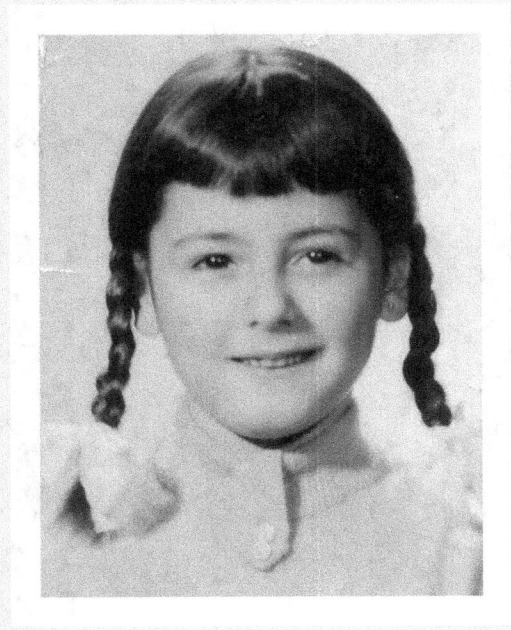

Emily Dickinson: 371

A precious—mouldering pleasure—'tis—
To meet an Antique Book—
In just the Dress his Century wore—
A privilege—I think—

His venerable Hand to take—
And warming in our own—
A passage back—or two—to make—
To Times when he—was young—

His quaint opinions—to inspect—
His thought to ascertain
On Themes concern our mutual mind—
The Literature of Man—

What interested Scholars—most—
What Competitions ran—
When Plato—was a Certainty—
And Sophocles—a Man—

When Sappho—was a living Girl—
And Beatrice wore
The Gown that Dante—deified—
Facts Centuries before

He traverses—familiar—
As One should come to Town—
And tell you all your Dreams—were true—
He lived—where Dreams were born—

His presence is Enchantment—
You beg him not to go—
Old Volumes shake their Vellum Heads
And tantalize—just so—

CHAPTER 19

COLORS

"I'm sorry but I have a problem with this. I need to return it. I don't want to, but it's just not right." It was 1959 and nine-year-old me was standing at the counter of a small store in Passaic, New Jersey. A few days earlier my Aunt Rae had given me my first ever giant box of crayons. My parents and I had lived in several different countries on two continents where I learned to speak and read in three different languages. But so many uprootings meant that large and cumbersome items like toys and crayons were not practical. So I never had many of either. I would sometimes share my friends' crayons or use them at school, but not at home.

When we moved to Passaic and near my Aunt Rae, she was quick to rectify that situation. I was spellbound. It was the biggest box of crayons I had ever seen, and it even had a built-in sharpener. I hugged my aunt gleefully and plotted how I would inaugurate my new tools. I loved playing school and would line up pencils and little bits of paper and some books on a table in front of me and write notes of some sort. All the accoutrements of school delighted me. This was going to join the group.

I pulled out the crayons one by one giggling at the names of the colors. Sepia! Burnt Sienna! Forest Green! What a marvel of colors and words this box held. But then I was stopped—taken aback. The color "Flesh" made no sense to me. It was a beige pinkish hue that bore little resemblance to some of my friends. I took it to my mother. "I think they called it that because that's the color of most people who buy these crayons," she started and then continued, "but it really doesn't represent a lot of the people we know, I agree."

It really didn't. My family fit this color well, but not my father's friend Kim, the Korean businessman who recently brought us a beautiful gift of an ancient scroll. Or Kajal, my mother's friend from India who taught her to make a delicious curry. Or many of my friends from Brazil.

I took my dilemma to a neighbor, Mrs. Cohen. She was very old and seemed wise. I thought she could help me. She told me that this was simply the way the world was. People in power make the decisions and they weren't always fair. People with this skin tone had the official "flesh color" and everyone else had to accept this.

I was stunned. "But that's not fair or kind or" my new favorite word "just," I sputtered. "Well, that's just the way it is and the less you think about it the happier you'll be. Just run along and play," she told me shooing me away.

I went home to my bedroom table where all of my school tools were lined up. I had been studying for my citizenship test and the Declaration of Independence was open right there by my crayons. "With liberty and justice for all," I read aloud. Clearly, as an almost citizen, I had to take matters into my own hands.

I didn't know where Aunt Rae had bought the Crayolas, but I guessed it was the small shop a few blocks away that seemed to have everything crammed into a tiny space.

Mr. Luigianno, with his deeply creased face, curly gray hair, and very hunched back was the owner, and he seemed to live behind the small, battered, wooden counter. I loved going in there and talking with him. I'd sit on a rickety stool that would magically appear, and he would tell me about his life growing up in Naples. "Ah, so beautiful," he'd often begin, "the sky a brilliant blue—the sun—Oh, it shines bright gold and warms the whole earth. And my mama's food—ach, I miss it so much. But here is good too. Angelina (his wife) and I have a good life here."

But today I had a complaint. "I'm sorry but I need to return this," I stated as I hesitantly and then with determination, pushed the glorious box toward him. "What's the matter, Sylvia? These are beautiful. Look, here is the sky. And here are the leaves of the trees in the springtime. Look!" I sighed and responded, "But Mr. Luigianno, a great error has been committed and I need to fix it. See this, it says "Flesh" but it doesn't mean it." He smiled softly as I continued, "I can't just do nothing. It's wrong."

Nodding with deep understanding, he responded: "How about I give you this big pack of paper in all these colors? Maybe you can use them?"

This seemed like a wonderful adjustment. I asked him if he would write to the Crayola company from his position as the owner of such an important store. Maybe they would listen to him. "Well, yes, I will do that, but if you really think something is wrong, you must be a good (future) citizen and speak up yourself. You must take one of these papers and write to the company and tell them. Explain clearly." This was a splendid idea, and I spent the next day writing and re-writing it, finally sending it on a Friday afternoon.

I never heard back from the company. Mr. Luigianno was as disappointed as I was, but over the next year we spent even more time laughing and telling stories—he of his beloved Naples, me of school and my family and my friends. "Life changes slowly," he would tell me, "until all of a sudden, POW, it's all different. You'll see. Change is coming."

When my family moved to New York City I made sure to put my exact address on a piece of bright blue paper so he would know where I was. We exchanged Christmas cards the next year or so, but then when I was twelve a letter came to me from Angelina. I opened it carefully and a small scrap of paper fell out. I picked it up and read the note: "My dear Josepe is very ill and cannot write. But he wanted me to send this to you and tell you that you made a difference. He wanted me to say that together we can make the world a better place for everyone. He also said the sky in Naples is cerulean." I smiled at the color reference and then looked at the scrap I was holding.

It was the paper from the "Flesh" crayon but now, in 1962, the company had changed the name. Now it said "Peach."

CHAPTER 20

CIRCLES

"It's today, it's today!" I exclaimed loudly and triumphantly, while shaking my mother awake. It was 1959 and I was nine years old. I knew of some older Jewish friends who were studying and practicing for Bar Mitzvahs and some Catholic friends who had Holy Communions. Neither was in my future. But I felt in my bones that today was going to be, like those rituals, the day that I would become something larger than myself. I was going to believe in something bigger than me. I was going to somehow expand in ever-larger concentric circles, into the world.

"OK, Sylvia," she said sleepily, "start getting ready. Your father will make the special pancakes you asked for and I promise I'll be ready to go soon." I carefully put on my new blue dress, tied a bright red ribbon around my pony-tailed hair, and very uncharacteristically made sure my white socks were pulled up to the same exact height on my legs. After breakfast we left the house with me twirling to the car, feeling the crisp December air on my face and seeing the last few brown leaves left on the trees waving to me gently.

I bounded into the courtroom and one of the officials, chuckling, had to ask me to slow down a bit. "I'm sorry," I sighed, addressing him, "but on a day like this it's especially hard to be calm. I'll try, though, because it's important." He laughed, asked my parents to take a seat, and then he walked with me to the front of the room.

"Your Honor," he began, "this young lady has passed all of the tests."

"I got everything completely right. Everything!" I blurted out.

The kindly judge looked amused and said, "Well, it appears this is very important to you. I'm very pleased."

"Important? It's more than that even," I began, "today is the whole new part of my life. It's like if I'm reading a book—I love books. Do you love books?" I saw him nod in understanding. "It's like a whole new chapter in my life. Today is a giant day."

He smiled and called me up to where he sat, God-like, on what I imagined to be a throne. In an action I much later learned was not standard or typical or required, he very ceremoniously asked me stand before him while he declared loudly, "I hereby state Sylvia Judith Kuhner to be a brand-new citizen of the United States of America." I felt my body almost quiver with happiness.

He extended his hand and said, "Let me be the first to welcome you." As he shook my small hand I stood tall and solemnly promised him that this country would be proud to call me a citizen. He looked me straight in the eye and said he was sure of it.

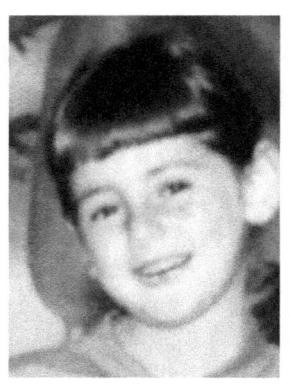

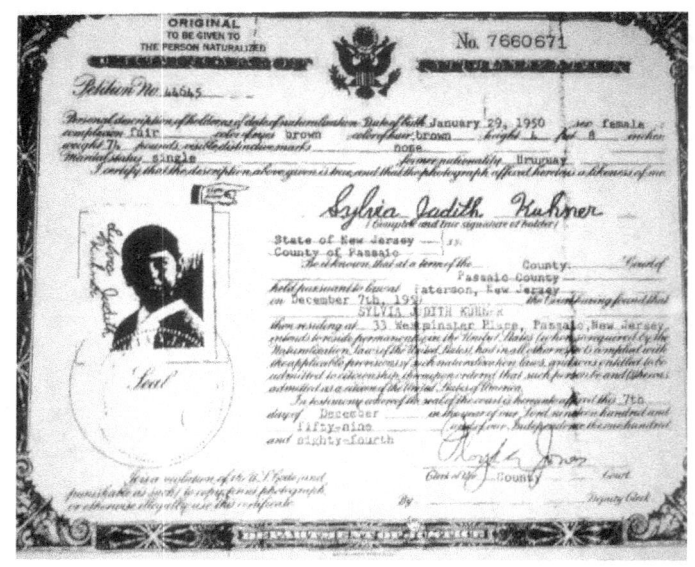

CHAPTER 21

SHOES

"Oh, I see that Mrs. Leary was in today," I exclaimed delightedly as I entered the store underneath the big Patrick O'Toole's Shoe Repair Shop sign. "Is her daughter doing any better yet?" Mr. O'Toole cut two slices of the home-made Irish soda bread on the counter, shook his head a sad "no" as he buttered the thick slices with creamy yellow butter, and handed me a piece.

While I ate he explained, "She was especially downcast today. Doctors don't think she's going to ever be able to walk again. Such sadness it is."

It was June 1960 and I was ten years old and living in Passaic, New Jersey. My dad had sent me to Mr. O'Toole's shop back in February with a pair of his damaged wing-tipped shoes to be fixed. I intended to just drop them off but instead got intrigued by some of the equipment in his shop. I asked a lot of questions and while I was there Mrs. Leary came in with a child-size shoe in a brace and a round loaf of bread which she placed on the counter.

She said, "Patrick, would you mind adjusting this for me please. Little Rose just can't manage that wobble there."

"Sure enough, Mary. Just let me get my tools," he responded. She looked over at me anxiously and in what seemed no more than a minute, he was done. "That'll hold her in tight. Thanks for the bread, Mary. Tastes just like me mother's it does!" he exclaimed. She smiled broadly and left into the cold winter afternoon.

"Mr. O'Toole, I think she forgot to pay," I helpfully pointed out. "No," he answered, "she paid me in bread. See, her daughter got polio a few years back and needs those braces. They don't have money for much these days, so she pays what she can."

I responded, "My grandmother did that at her store too. She made the most beautiful hats anywhere. People came from far away to buy them. But sometimes when someone really needed one and they couldn't pay, they would pay with something else." Then I giggled and told him the story of the live chicken Mrs. Tambores brought one time that chased my mother all through the store, out the door, and into the courtyard.

After that day, through the winter and spring and into summer, I stopped in to see him every few days. He loved telling me stories of his childhood in Ireland and of his dangerous and difficult voyage to America when he was only fifteen years old. "Aye. Lucky for me I learned this skill outside of Dublin. The whole family lost everything and my father apprenticed me when I was just twelve. Danny McCarthy was a good man, he was. Taught me everything."

And then Patrick O'Toole would tell me stories of the people he met and the lessons that Danny taught him. "Aye, one time a man, all raggedy and dirty, comes into his shop. I was ready to throw him out, I was, but Danny shakes his hand. 'Mr. Connors, how are you this fine morning?' he says to him and then continues, 'I see you be limping a bit. Can I have the honor of fixin' that shoe for you?' And wouldn't you know it, the man takes off his shoe and Danny takes care of it right there and gives it back and says, 'Thank you for coming in. See you again soon. Top o'the mornin' to ye.' And I turned to Danny and I asked him what that was all about. He told me Mr. Connors had been down on his luck since his wife died and slipped more and more into another world. No one could help much, but Danny says, he says to me, 'Patrick my boy, you got to do right by the world. You got to mend the world. Mend it one shoe at a time.' He taught me everything, that man."

I loved hearing his stories and being in his shop. Sometimes his little girl would come in from upstairs. I took to helping her with her kindergarten work. She was often coughing and tired and had missed so much of school that she was far behind. Her mother had two new babies to tend to and didn't have much time left for Katherine. I would sit with her on little benches in the corner of the store and teach her to sound out her letters and words. Sometimes I'd come with little stories I wrote using her new vocabulary. Mr. O'Toole would look over at us, delighted with his daughter's smiles and laughter and progress. He would tell me how she looked forward to my visits. "She's a smart one, you know. She's going to make us proud. She's getting stronger every day now."

The school year was almost over and at this point in our fifth-grade classroom Mrs. Jenkins was teaching us about different careers. This posed a great difficulty for me. I had no real skill or talent that I could measure. Like Janet, who was a wonderful dancer. Or Patty, whose mother made delicious homemade pasta and was teaching her that special skill. Or Ruth Ann, who could add and multiply and even divide in her head! I mused about my dilemma with Mr. O'Toole that afternoon. "I have no talent that I can think of," I told him while finishing the buttery bread. "But I want to do what your Mr. Danny McCarthy said. I want to mend the world. But I have no tools," I sighed.

Just then Katherine came bounding in and our afternoon of reading—she could read easy Golden Books now—and giggling began. As I left the store later, Mr. O'Toole told me to be sure to come next week on my very last day of school for the year. He wanted me to have something.

When I walked into his store the next Monday, Mr. O'Toole and his whole family were there to greet me. Katherine jumped up and down with excitement. "This is for you," she shouted, handing me a box. And beaming with pride she added, "I wrote the card all by myself!" Even the two babies were gurgling happily. Her mother hugged me and thanked me for helping out. "Katherine is so happy now. Her asthma is almost cured and she can sit and read on those days when it's too hard to play outside. It makes my heart so pleased to see her like that."

The note on top from Katherine said "Thank you. I Love You." I tore the newspaper wrapping paper and string off and found a beautiful brown box. Carved into the top was "Sylvia's Tools." I opened the lid to reveal pencils, a pen, and some chalk. "That's how you will mend the world, Sylvia," Mr. O'Toole said, smiling, "With stories and teaching and kindness. One shoe at a time. One shoe at a time."

CHAPTER 22

BOOKMOBILE

When I first spotted the bookmobile outside my sixth-floor apartment window, I thought it was a mirage. "Mirage" was a word I had discovered that day in one of my readings about deserts. It was 1961 and I was eleven years old and in love with words. Having lived in several countries, gone to schools there, and learned to read and write three different languages, words were like breathing to me—essential for life.

I grabbed my school bag and, too impatient to wait for the elevator, raced down the stairs. Miss Jones seemed to be waiting for me when I walked in. "Welcome," she said with a smile, "what can I help you find?"

"Books," I said. "I need books." Every Friday for months I stepped inside this cramped trailer filled with stories and poems and art. Miss Jones let me take out as many books as I could carry in my arms or in my school bag, and every week when I returned them I would tell her some new words I had learned. One week it was "life-line," another it was "interstellar." "Transcendence" stumped me, and she explained it's when you can rise above something that's going on right now and see it from a higher view.

Once Cousin Alma, a distant, older relative of my father, came to stay with us. "Down on her luck," my parents whispered. "She'll only be with us for a week." It was clear from the beginning I was not going to get along well with her. She questioned my book choices and complained to my parents that I ought not to be reading "such nonsense." My father, who had never restricted any of my readings, told her I'd be fine. But on Friday, her last day with us, she insisted on going with me to the bookmobile to see "what sort of people work there." I was delighted when she walked in, met Miss Jones, promptly walked out in a huff, and left me alone.

That was the day I found *Anne of Green Gables* on a shelf and discovered that it was Miss Jones' favorite book. I rushed home to read it and walked into a loud, angry confrontation between my parents and Alma. "How do you let her be influenced by *those* kind of people? Her skin was almost black. Black! They are not like us. They are filth," she was yelling. As my parents told her in no uncertain terms that such language—such words—and such attitudes were not welcome in our home, I listened through the walls of my bedroom.

Alma raced in, grabbed her suitcase, stuffed it hastily, and stormed out of our apartment and our lives.

That week I read *Anne of Green Gables* twice, running the words and sentences over my mind so that even my fingertips tingled with the sounds. When I saw Miss Jones that next Friday, I walked up the steps to the bookmobile, gave her an enormous hug, and told her my phrase for the week, which I had gotten from our favorite book: "kindred spirit" I said. "Like the two of us. We're kindred spirits."

CHAPTER 23

FIELD DAYS

"It doesn't say that girls aren't allowed. You should do this." It was 1961, I was eleven years old and in seventh grade. My friend Mary and I were in the hallway outside of the gym on a Monday afternoon looking at a sign-up sheet for spots on the relay team for next week's all-city field day. "Mary," I continued, "everyone knows you're the fastest runner in our whole class." It was true. Sometimes we would see her running around the neighborhood just for fun and if anyone needed something quick from the grocery store, they'd call Mary who would run there and back in no time.

"I don't ever remember a girl doing this—just because they don't exactly say 'no girls' doesn't mean that we can. Stuff like this has always been for boys," she said, her head bowed down. It made no sense to me. She continued, "If you want to do it, why don't you sign up?" In truth, running wasn't my passion. I liked fun silly games, but I didn't care about sports the way Mary did. She knew all the rules for football and even had a secret stash of baseball cards in a box under her bed. I never really cared about any of that.

"Look, field day sounds like loads of fun and see, tryouts are on Wednesday during math class. We don't have to go to math that day," I implored. Mary did not budge, so I put my own name on the list.

At tryouts I stood in a long line of boys in my required navy-blue gym bloomers and my white Keds sneakers. No one talked to me. When it was my turn to run against Henry Fisher, Mr. Arston once again re-stated the rules and looked at me. "Sylvia, do your best to keep up, OK? It's fine if you can't do this," he said, sighing. The whistle blew and off we went.

First I won against Henry Fisher, then Joey Sappriati, then five other boys. Eventually the tryouts were over and our team was decided. Three boys and me, a girl.

For the next two days kids in the hallways teased me and some were angry. "Stupid girl can't do this. You're going to lose for our whole school." And, "We thought we finally had a chance to win this year but you messed it all up. Dumb girl." And even, "I heard you're a foreigner. Go home. You can't come here and ruin our whole school."

"Ignore them," Mary admonished but continued, "I told you that girls don't do this. See what happens?"

I answered pleadingly, "But I won fair and square. I beat the others. I won. And Mary, you're so much faster than me— you should be doing this." She shook her head.

My mother was not happy about the situation either. It was difficult for her in 1961 to raise a strong-willed girl. From the time I was a toddler she told me that I needed to have my own career and not be dependent on anyone else, but the reality of the world in the 1950s and early '60s meant she also wanted me to marry and have the security of a husband. It was a tension that caused us both confusion. She did not, however, want me in the field day competition. She was clear. "If you win, no boy will ever like you. It's just not . . . not . . . not feminine. How will it look?" I kept explaining that I qualified. It was clear. But no one heard me.

Mrs. Harrison saw me sitting by myself on Sunday afternoon in the playground. She lived by herself in apartment 2B and I had seen her several times struggling with carrying groceries with her left arm while using her cane with the right and so I had helped her. Her apartment was full of old things—sepia-toned photos in elaborate gold frames, teapots with roses and irises painted on the side, a brown velvet couch, tapestries on the walls, and, my favorite, a very old wind-up dog toy that twisted and circled on his small round faded red ball.

On that Sunday she sat next to me. "Are you OK, Sylvia?" she asked, her blue eyes sincere and kind. So I blurted out my dilemma and confusion in one long stumbling monologue. When I was finished, she sighed deeply. "You know, I always wanted to be a doctor. I could have been a good one, I'm sure of it. But I never saw women doctors anywhere and my fiancé, Jerry, thought it was a silly idea. He wanted to get married and start a family. I wanted that too. But, still, I wanted to be a doctor. I never told my dreams to anyone else because they would laugh. So I married Jerry. He went off to war in 1917 and was killed."

I never knew this about her. She continued, "Maybe I should have gone back to school. I have thought about it a lot, but I was too timid. I worked at sales counters in department stores for thirty years—retired a few years back when my legs couldn't take the standing up anymore." She smiled and continued, "I can't tell you what to do, but I can tell you to not let your own heart down because you will live with it your whole entire life."

She patted my hand and we walked back into the building and up the elevator together.

On Monday we had field day. On the bus I heard jeers and accusations from a lot of the kids. Teachers were quick to quiet them, but they kept welling up. My legs and arms felt shaky, and I wasn't at all sure I'd be able to even walk, much less run.

In the giant Forest Hills arena there were hundreds of kids from all over the city yelling and cheering for their schools. When it was time for our school to join the competition I went out onto the field with my teammates and, suddenly oddly calm, simply waved to the crowd. We set up in relay team position, the whistle blew, and off we went. Round one. Round two. And, finally, Round three.

That year, for the first time ever, our school placed in the championships: silver medal. We came in second in the entire city. Suddenly we were all heroes. "Sylvia, you were great. Grabbed that baton and ran, ran, ran like the wind," Jeremy gushed. Sandra and Ruthie and Rhonda and Paul echoed that. The following day there was an official assembly at school where we stood tall on the stage in front of everyone, our pins were given to us, and the whole school cheered.

I told Mrs. Harrison that afternoon and she hugged me and cried.

The following year five girls were in the tryouts and two were on the team, Mary and me. We won again. My mother tried not be encouraging, but she could not hide her smile. My proud father wrote in my eighth-grade graduation book: "One's life is a history book written on time instead of paper and with character instead of ink."

Mary's passion continued through her life. She became a gym teacher and, eventually, the coach of a women's college soccer team. My interests led me elsewhere. But about twelve years ago, in my late fifties, I took up tennis. It was unexpected. "Are you sure you want to do that at 'your age?,' I heard. Yes, yes, I was sure. And my husband of forty years said, "Have fun and enjoy it!" And I have.

June 24, 1953

To my darling Sylvia,
This graduation marks
the end of "Chapter I."
One's life is a history book
written on time instead of
paper and with character
instead of pen and ink.
May all the following
chapters be as full of happiness
and joy as this first one.
Deepest love
Your Father

CHAPTER 24

COMMUNITY

"Wow, you've really made a lot of progress here," I told him as I ran my hands along the uneven, cold gray rocks. It was 1961, I was eleven years old, and we were visiting my father's father, Grandpa Kuhner, in New England. Periodically, we'd make the tense four-hour trip up to his house from our apartment in New York City traveling first through crowded streets, then highways, and then winding country roads. My parents did not understand my grandfather's new way of life. After a very successful career as an engineer with many international patents and lots of distinguished awards, he had retired to a hundred acres of rough, wooded, and pond-filled land in central Massachusetts. To make matters more confusing for my parents, he was determined to carve out the land himself—chopping and hauling lumber to make a ramshackle hut to live in while a larger house (which he designed) was being built. And the stones—those multi-sized boulders that seemed to grow, weed-like, from the land he was plowing for vegetable gardens and foundations—which he began using for a wall were beyond comprehension for their cosmopolitan sensibilities.

"Sara, please," my father would implore of my mother on our way there, "don't bring up his age again. I know you worry about his health, but he's strong and bringing that up will only make him angry." I knew he was saying that not just to her but to himself as well. These visits were difficult for all of them. In truth my grandfather, who had worked in a corporation all of his adult life, steadily increasing in rank and success by his focus and dedication to a single career, could not understand my dad's choice to be a globe-trotting entrepreneur with a dizzying roller-coaster of finances. My father took chances that my grandfather did not understand. They were very different in many ways.

But I loved my visits there. My dad would glide me about the cleared-out pond in a canoe, and then, as an adventure, we'd slide under the rickety bridge and paddle around the adjacent muck-filled one. I'd often wander alone all over the woods with the small binoculars my grandpa had gotten for me dangling from the strap around my neck, ready for sightings of birds or critters or unusual leaves. I'd always come back to the house with visual treasures which Grandpa would have me describe in great detail. At first he had asked me to draw things I saw, but I was hopelessly incapable of capturing things in pictures. I could, though, use words and he encouraged my verbal paintings.

When he first started to build the stone wall a few years back in 1958, I had watched him carefully. He would haul rocks in a wheelbarrow and lay them out side-by-side on the ground. Then he picked out one or two and began piling them atop one another. Slowly he continued using them all—wedging one here and one there, pulling this one to the side and placing it farther down the structure. It was a long, difficult process. I watched.

This visit, in June 1961, was different. We'd been living in Brazil for almost two years and had not seen him all that time. His new house was now built and had marvels like heated floors and remote controls for windows and appliances, all of which he had designed himself. He showed me everything while my parents busied themselves with unpacking and sorting details. I was delighted with the contraptions, but I wanted most of all to see the progress of the stone wall. "It's marvelous!" I exclaimed as I ran my hand along it using my new favorite phrase, "simply marvelous."

He chuckled at my gleefulness. "Well, it really is a bit of a marvel when you think about it," he began, "but it took a lot of work and figuring out too."

I agreed with him and said, "I remember watching you do this—it seemed hard. And now look how beautiful it is. But it's not finished yet is it?" We both looked to our left where there was still an empty space.

"Not yet," he began, "but soon it'll be done."

"Then what will you do?" I asked, imaging possible larger projects.

"I think there will be a lot of tending to my creation here," he sighed and continued, "sometimes things shift and need to be adjusted. But really, if it's done well—done solidly—it should last a long, long time. Hundreds of years ago people built these types of walls and they're still standing today." Until that very moment I had not considered the history of the land. I had not thought about actual people living on the land. I had learned some history in school, but it seemed very remote—not about actual people but about events I would never understand.

I stood back and looked at the whole almost-finished wall and had a sudden thought. "Grandpa, wait right here—I'll be right back." I ran inside and searched my little bag of treasures that traveled with me everywhere, grabbed what I needed, and ran back out to his side. Breathlessly I opened a map. Several years ago, when we first came to the United States and landed in Texas, my American father had decided to show us our new land by driving us to California and then across the entire country to New York. We spent weeks on the roads. There were few interstate highways in 1957 so the only way to be guided was with maps. My mom was happier in the back, so I sat with my dad in the front seat and acted as his co-pilot. Our handy Esso maps were perfect. I loved trying to read the names of the towns and cities and states, running my fingers over the blue lines and the red lines with road numbers, and helping to direct our journey. I carried my maps for years afterward—opening them and tracing routes, then closing them securely.

"Look, Grandpa," I said as I showed him my map of the country, "if you look at all the parts of it, together it's like looking at the rocks. The states and towns—they're all different sizes and shapes, but somehow they fit together and make one whole structure. And all the people all over the country are so different, but together it works."

He took a moment and looked from the map to the rocks and then his gaze landed on me. "Hmmmm, I can see it," he began. "You know," he continued in his thick German accent, "both of us are immigrants. We have both come to this country from somewhere else. And we are part of its history now. All of us—every kind of person of every color from every kind of background and every kind of worship—all of us. And every single stone, every single person, is a valuable part of the whole structure, isn't it?" He tapped the rocks with his fingers and looked out to our car parked nearby and then looked back at me and continued. "But you know what? Even when it looks finished, the country, the world, your life, this stone wall—they all need to keep being adjusted and fixed. You need to give attention to it. But you know that if it was built well and sturdily, and it will last long into history. All of it."

He hugged me, I folded my map, and we went inside for dinner. There were no disagreements and no arguments throughout the entire visit. On the way home my father exclaimed that it was the best time he had ever spent with his dad. Two years later, Grandpa finished the stone wall. In 1979 I traveled with my new baby daughter from my home in Maryland to visit him and to have her sit on the wall which she patted delightedly with her small pink hand. "I've had to shore up a piece here and there," he told me, "but it's holding up strong." Three years later he died, in his bed, looking out over his land and the stones.

My daughter and grandsons now live in central Massachusetts near where he had lived. One of the boys loves maps and the other loves building things. With their mom's help, they have taken up painting small rocks and placing them all around their neighborhood and town for others to discover and be delighted.

CHAPTER 25

GREEN

"Mom, I'm going downstairs to tell them about the dance practice." It was 1962, I was twelve years old and living in an apartment building in New York City. My friends were coming over the next day after school to practice some new dances we'd seen on *American Bandstand*–especially "The Mashed Potatoes." We were a noisy bunch and generally gathered at Ruthie's house. But tomorrow was my turn. I thought the polite thing to do was to let Mrs. Green, who lived directly below us in 5L, know ahead of time. I didn't know her or her husband very well, but I had met them in the elevator a few times. Mrs. Green, with her thick German accent, curly gray hair, and bright blue eyes, looked and sounded a lot like my grandmother Annette who I had left behind in Uruguay when my family moved to the United States four years ago.

She died two years later, and truth was, I still missed her. And my grandfather, Max.

When Mrs. Green opened her door, she looked scared and shaky. "Come in, dear," she began, "I'm just waiting for an important phone call." I walked with her to the big yellowish armchair with doilies barely covering its worn arms and back. I sat on the floor next to her.

"What happened? Are you OK?" I asked, wondering if I should call someone for help.

"No, I'll be fine. I just need to get my mind off of it until the call comes. Tell me something about yourself. Tell me a story," she pleaded with her voice and her eyes, and continued, "Did you ever have to wait for news?"

I hung my head down and began, "I can tell you about last week." And so I explained how by accident I learned that my beloved grandfather had died a whole year ago and no one ever told me. How I searched the mail for weeks for a letter from him and none came. And finally, my parents gave me the letter from our relative in Montevideo explaining it all. "I was so angry," I said looking up at Mrs. Green's eyes, "because he died, because I didn't know, because they kept such a big secret from me."

She looked down at me and said, "Ay, schatzi," she began with a sigh, "sometimes things are kept from us because others think it will be too much for us. Sometimes they think the truth is so big that it might swallow us up."

I nodded in agreement and continued, "My mom told me that after my grandmother died I was so upset that she couldn't stand to tell me about my grandfather."

Mrs. Green sighed and swept her hand about the room, "Look around here." I suddenly noticed the faces and hands and landscape paintings jamming the expansive whiteness of the walls. She continued, "I painted all of these from my memory. It's all I have—my memory—of my homeland and my family."

She told me the story of how in Germany as a young woman she saw children and families herded into trucks and trains. She asked her parents what was happening, and they did not tell her. She saw her father taking down all symbols of their Jewish religion—the mezuzah by the door, the menorah on the mantle—but they did not explain. When the banging on the door came and she, her baby brother, and her parents were shipped to Dachau and separated, no one said what would happen.

Now she looked up at her paintings, "They divided us up—sent me away again. They found I could paint and draw, so I worked in a big room making Nazi posters. Nazi posters. My art talent saved my life, but look what I had to do with it to survive."

Now she was in tears, but she continued, "When the tanks rolled in and I saw that American flag I thought it was the most beautiful thing in the world. People had come to save us. To save us. That's when I met Jimmy."

"Oh," I interjected, "Mr. Green!"

She smiled. "Yes. It was the worst time of my life and then it became the best. We fell in love. He brought me here."

"What happened to your family?" I asked, hopefully.

"They were all killed right away. No one was left but me.

And so I started painting my memories as soon as I could. It was all I had, but it was a lot. The more I painted the more I could bring them all back to me." I looked around. Even my twelve-year-old eyes could see the vividness of the colors, the clarity and precision on the hands, the hair, the eyes of the people on her walls. "Ay, Liebchen," she said, "art saved my life many times. It saves me now."

The sudden ringing of the black phone by her chair startled us both. She picked up the heavy receiver and nodded as she listened. I stood up and walked around the room looking at the memories and remembering my own grandparents. When she hung up the phone, I went back to her. "Is it OK?" I asked.

"No," she stated frankly. "It is not. The results of the tests are not good. My health is not good." Right then Mr. Green came through the front door jauntily and stopped suddenly when he saw his wife's face. "Gertie?" he asked—he pleaded. I knew I was invading a private moment and quickly left.

Ruthie agreed to have the dance event at her house the next day. I stopped in frequently to see Mrs. Green over the next few weeks. By the end, she could not leave her bed. A month after her death Mr. Green began moving out of apartment 5L. "I'll go to Michigan to live with my sister and her family," he told me when I saw him in the elevator. "I'm packing all of those paintings so carefully. I want my nieces to know these memories—these stories. Did I ever tell you how I met my Gertie?" We were now on the fifth floor, and we both got out and walked to the apartment where movers were wrapping and storing things. He began, "She was in Dachau concentration camp. When our Army division arrived to liberate them, the people there looked like ghosts. They were so thin and weak and afraid. Many threw themselves on the ground and wept. We gave them food and they took it and hid it in their shirts or pants—afraid it would disappear. But not Gertie. I saw her, a woman who could barely walk and was carrying paint brushes in her hands, take the bread, smile, thank us and break it in two pieces, giving half to some small child who was holding her leg and crying. I had never seen such kindness in my life." Now Mr. Green was crumpled in a lone chair by the door.

He continued, "She never spoke ill of anyone. But she wanted to keep the story of her family alive, and she wanted to remember beauty, and kindness, and humanity, and love. So she painted. What art do you have in your heart, Sylvia?" he asked. No one had ever asked me that before.

"I can't paint, I can't sing, I can barely dance. I don't think I have any." I answered sadly. And then I brightened, "I love words. I can paint with them and tell stories!" He smiled. "If you give life to people you love, people you meet, people who you care about, the stories will give you life. Art keeps the world alive."

EMILY DICKINSON: 292

If your Nerve, deny you—
Go above your Nerve—
He can lean against the Grave,
If he fear to swerve—

That's a steady posture—
Never any bend
Held of those Brass arms—
Best Giant made—

If your Soul seesaw—
Lift the Flesh door—
The Poltroon wants Oxygen—
Nothing more—

CHAPTER 26

MISSILES

Over the loudspeaker we heard the principal's urgent voice: "This is not a drill. This is an emergency. Everyone out into the hall and use the techniques we've practiced." And then very loudly, "Now!"

It was mid-October 1962, I was twelve years old and in the eighth grade at PS 63 Queens, New York, and our country was engulfed in the Cuban Missile Crisis. Our teachers had been drilling us for days on various survival techniques, mainly "duck and cover" and "hide under the desks," because it was widely assumed that nuclear bombs were aimed at us in our city as the first line of attack. We all felt powerless. But today, right now, this was even worse. We were in the hallway—a new and more terrifying maneuver. We all filed out quickly, sat on the cold floor, were reminded to keep our backs to the wall and to sit very still. In the cavernous silence, I looked around tentatively and saw heads bowed, prayers mumbled, tears being wiped away.

I too was filled with sadness and fear for the world, for myself, and for my family. Just a month ago my normally active and energetic father had undergone serious surgery from which he almost did not recover. He was finally home now, but languishing in pain. My mother spent her days fretting over his slow recovery and also the panic of what most believed would be imminent bombings. And now here I was on the cold, gray linoleum, shivering with terror about my demise and facing the possibility of never seeing my parents again.

The anxiety on our faces prompted our history teacher, Mrs. Rothman, who had led us out to our spots and was now sitting on the opposite side of the hall and facing us, to address us in a quiet, but firm voice. We hung on every word desperate for any solace we could find. She began: "Shortly after we were married, my husband fought in World War II. After it was over and he came home he didn't talk about it much, but I knew it had been horrible for him and others. He still had some shrapnel in his chest from a particularly dangerous mission which I knew caused him a great deal of pain. But still, I would see him really enjoying a simple slice of pie or the sight of a brightly colored bird on our windowsill in ways I didn't see before. Every day when he left for his job as a bus driver, he would hug me and say what a beautiful day it was—even if it was raining."

She took a deep breath as we heard battalions of planes roaring above us—we all looked up. Then silence, and she continued: "One day I asked him why he was so . . . well, so appreciative of everything. So many others were angry or distressed. And he told me: 'After I was shot I figured out that things like this—like this terrible, terrible war—either make you better or worse when you come out of it. I set myself on trying to come out of this a better person. I decided that I was going to really enjoy life because this experience would teach me a valuable lesson. So I was going to be better for it.'"

As we sat there scared and shivering, I hung on her every word, hoping for some balm to fill my breaking heart. She finished, "So, when this ordeal—our ordeal right now—is done and we all go back to our regular lives, think about whether this will make you a better person or a worse one. Decide that now inside of yourself, because it will matter for your whole life."

And as she finished, the siren sounded the "all clear" and we were dismissed for lunch. Kids scampered to the cafeteria, but I bolted out the door, ran across a highway, over a busy avenue, rounded the corner, and breathlessly entered the lobby of my apartment building. I knew it was foolish at the time, but my overwhelming fear and anxiety just took over. I found my mother crying in the kitchen and my father on the couch listless and very pale.

"This will make us stronger," I vowed loudly as I burst into our apartment. "We will get through this—all of it—and it will teach us how much we love each other and how strong we can really be." Of course, they were shocked by this, but I had a very firm resolve. And even though I loved being at school, I stayed home to help and to just be with the two people I so dearly loved. Several days later the missile crisis was over, my father's health began to improve, and my mother's panic began to abate. And, indeed, we really were never again the same as before the crisis.

We were better.

CHAPTER 27

LOVE FIELD
(OR, HISTORY LESSON)

I was thirteen, and it was Friday, November 22, 1963. As I walked into class I tripped over my own feet, stumbled, caught myself right before falling over, and then tumbled into my seat, giggling uncontrollably. "I was sure you were going down for the count," my friend Helen laughingly stated. Judy looked over at me and in her instructive way—she was always trying to make the rest of us have more poise—explained to me that if I just stood up straighter, my body alignment would allow more grace in my walking.

"Oh, Judy," I blurted out between fits of giggles, "I think it's pretty hopeless. My feet just keep growing so fast that my brain can't keep up with it." She sighed and turned her perfectly attentive gaze to the front of the room where our teacher was supposed to be sitting.

We were in Miss Kelsey's English class. But she was late. She was never late. Something must have happened, because she was absolutely clear about expectations, and being on time was essential. "You can't control a lot in this world," she would tell us repeatedly, "but you can control how you respond to events. And being on time gives you the opportunity to show how responsible you are." Last month in the many spirited class discussions about the first book of the semester, Dickens' *Great Expectations,* she led us over and over to the understanding that so many events in our lives are totally out of our control. "Things happen that you don't anticipate or want, but those events don't define who you are. How you respond to them is what truly matters. That's where your choices are; that's where the real *you* happens."

I wondered a great deal about the main character, Pip, in that massive novel, and the many events that befell him, and all the choices he made. I thought about my own life also.

I felt especially lucky that fall. The leaves on the grounds of our rural Massachusetts boarding prep school were an especially glorious spectacle for me, a city girl. I was surrounded by friends, looking forward to fun weekend activities, and delighted by having access to all the books I could possibly want in our (to my mind) perfect library. I loved everything about my new country, the world, and the entirety of the universe. Possibilities abounded.

But this day when the usually punctual and pleasant Miss Kelsey walked into class late, she was clutching a handkerchief. And even from the third row back I could see her eyes were red and puffy. She started to speak but had to stop to let the catch in her throat subside. And then: "President Kennedy has been shot. He landed in Love Field, Dallas, was in a motorcade, and an assassin shot him. He is presumed dead. Dead. Dead." At this she held onto the side of the wide oak desk she had been standing next to, and continued, "We will know more details later."

Our room was silent.

The rest of the class was a blur.

On my solitary walk back to the dorm after class—the bright sky above me, the crinkly brown leaves under my feet, the brisk air stroking my cheeks—I was stunned. I didn't believe the president was shot. How could I? Love Field was where I landed when I first arrived in the United States six years earlier. Love Field—it was to me a perfect name for the beginning of my world in this new country that I so cherished—that represented endless possibilities for the future. Love.

But on that day the reality of human nature's capacity not only for greatness, but also for harm, became astoundingly clear. This. This can happen. How do we understand the immensity of this horror? Teachers talked to us. We talked to each other. Nothing helped.

By Sunday I realized that I had not read the book due for Monday's English class. That life really was going to continue. "It's not what happens but how you deal with it that shows your nature," echoed over and over in my mind.

I did my work and life did continue. The world continued.

The country continued. It has marched along on winding twisting paths. But for me, that day was the beginning of an awareness not just of the evil that can befall a man or a nation. It was also the realization that I had to balance whatever horrors happened with good. My purpose in life had to be, *to be a force for good.* The assigned book that I read for that Monday's class? The novel, "Cry, the Beloved Country."

CHAPTER 28

PATTERNS

"This is the pattern we will all follow," our teacher, Mrs. Carlisle, told us as she held up a Simplicity pattern number 4972 envelope. It was late February 1963 and here, in our Home Economics Class, in Public School 63 in New York City, we were starting the work of sewing our eighth-grade graduation dresses. She carefully explained the process we would be following over the next several months as we worked once a week on our projects, and then instructed us in how to take precise measurements. "Now girls, be sure to go to the store and get the right size pattern."

As we left the room chattering excitedly, I noticed that Sally Ann stayed behind to talk to the teacher. She looked worried. She was the smartest girl in the entire grade, always winning spelling bees and geography games, but she could never go over to anyone's house after school because she had to help out at home. Her mother was overwhelmed with Sally Ann's five young brothers and sisters, and she constantly had to help. She seemed generally cheerful about this except for one time. That was the day, a few weeks back, when we had a special event after school where a famous writer came to talk to us. But she couldn't stay. "Got to go help at home. My dad's in a bad way and mom just can't do any more," she told us sadly.

"You know her dad's a drunk, don't you?" Ruthie told me when we walked home. I did not. She continued, "He used to be an electrician, but something happened and he lost his job so now he drinks all the time. They keep getting poorer and poorer. My mom says it's a real shame how they have to live."

Now I waited for Sally Ann to finish talking to Mrs. Carlisle. She looked sad when she came out into the hall. "Are you OK?" I asked her. "Yes," she sighed, "I'm fine, just sort of tired." We walked silently together to English class.

My mother had no interest in sewing and no understanding of the process, so I went to the fabric store on my own that afternoon. I pulled out the drawer with the appropriate number on the card displayed in the front, and immediately found the pattern in my size. The dizzying amount of instructions made me appreciate that I'd have a teacher to guide me along. I paid the 65 cents and excitedly wandered through the fabrics. In a few weeks we would get to pick those out—but not yet. Our dresses were required to be white, but we could each choose our own fabric and our color for the cummerbund.

The next week we filed into Home Ec and sat at our designated sewing tables. My partner was Sally Ann and

I excitedly chatted with her about the fabric store. Then I noticed she didn't bring her pattern. "Oh, I didn't have time to go," she explained. This was odd because the store was right around the corner from her house.

The teacher started class and asked each of us to hold up our pattern envelopes and turn them to the back where the requirements were listed. "You'll see the precise amount of fabric and the various notions you'll need—thread, zipper, buttons. Look at those carefully as I come around to help you." Chattering began as heads pored over the details. Mrs. Carlisle came over to us first and said, "Sally Ann, I was hoping you'd do me a favor. As it turns out I made a mistake and got the wrong size and since I opened it, I can't return it. Can you please use this one? I think it might be your size." As she handed her the envelope Sally Anne's face lit up and her blond curls bounced as she excitedly said, "This is perfect!"

Class continued. We learned to determine exactly what we would need. Then the instructions were to go to the store to have the fabric for the next week.

After school I walked to the fabric store with Ruthie and Amy and Betty. "I think Mrs. Carlisle gave Sally Ann the pattern on purpose. I think maybe she didn't have the money to buy it," Ruthie said. I hadn't thought about this. What would she do? Fabric was expensive and so were all those notions.

"Do you know her mom is going to have another baby? My mom says that they're having trouble feeding everyone," Betty continued.

"How is she going to be able to have a dress for graduation? This is a terrible situation. We need to figure this out," I stated. By the time we got to the store we had hatched a plan. The next week we put it into operation.

"Mrs. Carlisle is going to be so mad at me," I whispered to Sally Ann a few days later. "I bought twice the amount of fabric I should have. I read the envelope wrong. She's going to think I'm stupid. Can I just cut it in half and give you the extra part? I don't want her to know."

She beamed. "Sure. That would be great. It'll save me the trouble of going to the store." And so, for the next several weeks we continued laying out the patterns and pinning them, cutting and basting, giggling and measuring. An extra zipper was found on the floor in the back and buttons were plentiful when we all put them in a box and picked a few we liked.

Slowly and surely we sewed and created our dresses, carefully following the rules laid out for us—carefully following the patterns. By the end of May we were almost finished. The fabric for our cummerbunds was all we had left to get, and our own personal color was a very significant choice. "Sally Ann," Amy asked, "what's your favorite color?"

"Oh, I love pink so much," she declared.

Amy, whose clear choice was always yellow, declared that pink was hers too and continued: "Wow! Great. My aunt says she's going to treat me to that fabric. I'll get some for you too. Save you the trip."

Our dresses were finished just in time and Mrs. Carlisle was proud of all of them. "You girls are so beautiful," she told us, "and not just because of the dresses. Dresses are important, following patterns and learning to sew are important skills, but real beauty comes from inside your soul. You are beautiful, girls. Remember that."

At graduation the next week we all filed into the auditorium in our dresses feeling very grown-up. We took our seats and at the end of the program filed out into the cafeteria where there were tables of cookies and Hawaiian punch. I was surprised to see Sally Ann's mother there with all five little kids. They surrounded her excitedly, tugging at her dress and dancing around. My parents waved to me from the back of the room and as I headed there, Sally Ann's mom stopped me. "Oh, don't you girls look so lovely!" she gushed, and continued, "we're all so proud of our girl. She's so smart. And look how you all sewed your dresses! And the school giving all of you all the fabric and necessities for free. So generous of them to do that for all of you."

I saw my friend look down and I quickly responded, "I know! We're so lucky!" Sally Anne hugged me while fiercely wiping away some tears. And as I walked away and toward my parents, I heard her mom call out, "You are all so beautiful."

The following year I went to a boarding prep school in New England and as happens, I lost touch with many of my early schoolmates. Every now and then I would hear about one or the other of them. The late sixties and then the seventies were turbulent times for the country and for us all. Time marched on. The eighties. The nineties. And then, a few years ago I heard from Betty. She had just settled into a retirement community in Florida and while clearing out her old home had found some pictures from our eighth-grade graduation, which she sent me via email. I was delighted and called her immediately. After getting caught up on our own lives, I asked her if she knew anything about Sally Ann's life.

"Well, she had a pretty hard time of it. Helped her mom raise her brothers and sisters, and right after high school worked day and night so they could all go to college and trade schools. But, wouldn't you know it, when she was fifty-five years old, she herself went to college. Got a scholarship and everything. Graduated in just three years. Then she kept going. And now she's going to get her PhD. In philosophy. Imagine that. At our age!" she chuckled delightedly into the phone, and then continued, "Told me the title of her dissertation but I didn't understand all those words. So, she explained to me that she researched and studied what beauty is. I didn't remember anything about this, but she said Mrs. Carlisle and we girls were the first to help her learn the true definition of that word."

And she finished, "Beauty. Imagine that!"

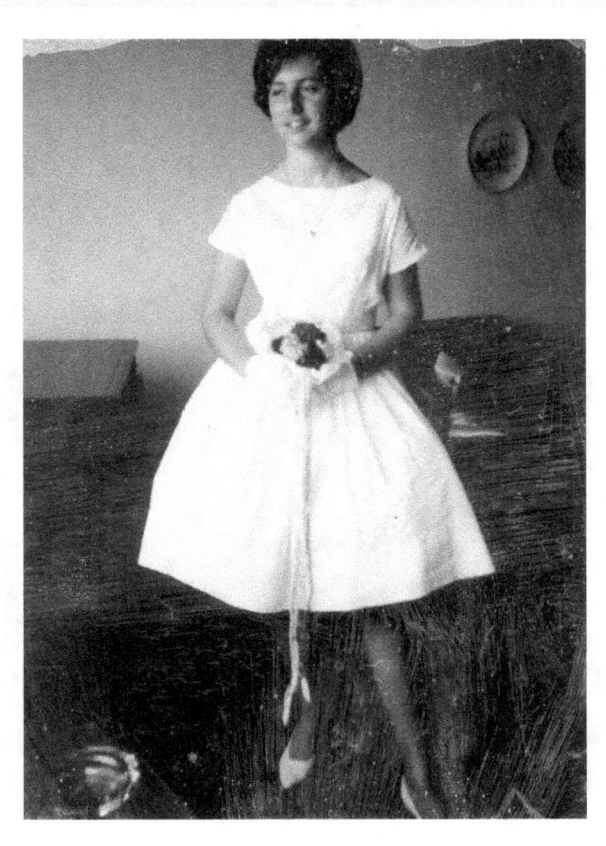

CHAPTER 29

SOARING

"Jimmy, I'm asking you for help. Right now. I need help. Sylvia is really hurt." Incapable of fully grasping them, I could hear Joshua saying these words through a vague echo in my ears as they swirled aimlessly in my mind. It was late August 1963, I was thirteen years old, and lying on the concrete ground under the swings in the play area of our New York City apartment complex.

Joshua was three years younger than I was. He had a lot of challenges, both physical and speech-based, and since the family's move to our area three months ago his anxious parents trusted me to babysit him often. "You have a real knack for talking to him," his mom began just this morning, "and I've seen his confidence grow this summer. He starts sixth grade in two weeks and . . ." her voice trailed off as she wrung her hands.

"Don't worry, Mrs. Kafitz," I began, "I really think he's going to find his way. I've seen him understand more and more every day. Today we're going to the playground where all the kids from his grade go. I'll be sure to help him get along."

When he was a baby, Joshua had contracted polio. It had left him with a pronounced left-sided limp, stuttering language, and large thick-lensed glasses, all of which seemed to make him an easy target for some of the other boys in his new neighborhood. He had avoided them by staying inside feigning illness or an exaggerated love of board games. Slowly we had ventured out; first to the nearby park, and then to the empty schoolyard of PS 63 Queens where he'd go in September and where I'd just graduated from the eighth grade. I knew the place well. "Look up there. That's the window of the principal's office. Right there on the first floor. And over there is where the science classes are."

He smiled at that. Joshua's great love was science, and he had told me over and over how one day he was going to be a doctor. "I'm going to cure the world of all the diseases," he'd smile. "Well, maybe not all of them. But I'm going to make a start!"

On one of our last days of the summer together we talked about Dr. Jonas Salk while eating bright orange popsicles on a park bench at the edge of the playground. That researcher who had created the polio vaccine was his hero. "He doesn't even know most of the kids he kept from getting polio," he began while quickly glancing down at his left leg, "still he helped them," he exclaimed.

I chimed in as he wiped orange ice from his chin, "Know what I think? I think most people really want to help other people. Sometimes they get caught up in their own worries or fears or even fears about themselves, and then they act self-ishly or, sometimes, even cruelly. But mainly people want to help." Joshua nodded hesitantly.

The next morning we went to the playground. Jimmy and his friends were on the far corner, huddled together laughing, playfully grabbing a basketball from each other and bouncing and dodging to and away in what looked like a choreographed modern dance. Their loud yells pierced the air and made Joshua cringe with anxiety. We sat on two nearby swings and as I started to pump my legs pushing mine higher, he laughed with glee. I went soaring, feeling the rush of the almost-September wind in my face—remembering that in one short week I'd be off for my high school beginnings at a boarding school in far-off Massachusetts, and loving the essence of it all. I smiled down at the delighted Joshua and then, suddenly losing my bearings, suddenly losing my entire sense of time and space, I tumbled head-first onto the cold, gray ground.

Joshua called my name and I heard him but was power-less to speak. And as I tried to raise myself up, I saw him shuffle and limp toward Jimmy and I heard his commands. The group of boys quickly came to my aid. One of them rushed to get their mom, who was a nurse, another got a bunch of sweatshirts for my head to lie on, one got me water from a nearby hose, and one grabbed Mr. Carter the building superintendent in his basement office. Joshua sat with me, talking calmly and reassuringly.

Later the doctor said I had a concussion and needed to rest, but everyone's quick actions saved me from greater harm.

The following week I went off to boarding school.

When I came home for a visit several weeks later, Joshua was one of my first visitors. "So, how was living away?" he wanted to know. I described the countryside and cows I'd seen and how the leaves were beginning to turn colors. "I know how that happens," he began, delighted to share his science knowledge with me. "It's when the temperature gets cold and there's less light, the leaves stop making chlorophyll which is the stuff that makes them green." I nodded. And then I asked him about his new school and the kids. He began, "Well, I don't really have too many friends yet. There's one kid I play chess with during recess and there's one kid in the eighth grade who's going to start a science club. And there's Jane, who really likes rocks and microscopes."

Then he continued, "And Jimmy. Well, he's not like a friend or anything. I mean he doesn't do stuff that I do. But you know what? The very first day in the cafeteria when I took my tray to an empty table, I spilled my milk all over." Oh, now my heart cried out for poor Joshua alone, limping to his table alone on his first day in a new school, and then (I could feel it in my bones!) the horror of that accident. He continued, "Right away there was Jimmy with a whole handful of paper towels. He helped me clean it all up. No one laughed or anything. Then a couple of other kids came over and sat down with me and he went back to his friends."

I was holding back tears. He continued, "I think that after you fell, I found out that you were right. Most people really want to help. Even when they're way different from you. Even when they don't really know you. So, I'm not so afraid anymore." He hugged me goodbye and had one more thought to share: "I think that sometimes people are like leaves. When they have very difficult circumstances, they change colors. You can see the gold inside that's actually what they are. That's when they become really beautiful."

CHAPTER 30

LIFE AND DEATH

"I come up here to think about life a lot," I told him as we both looked out at the Connecticut River from our high perch. It was 1965, I was fifteen years old, and my grandmother and her third and best husband, Lieberson, were visiting me at my boarding prep school, Northfield School for Girls, in Massachusetts.

"Ah, my Lieber," she said to me when they were first married just a few years earlier—both of them in their 60s—"he's such a good man and so intelligent. Anything he doesn't know he goes and looks it up. He reads everything. He's interested in everyone. I'm so lucky to have such a husband so late in life." And then, with a gleam in her eyes and a smile that dimpled her cheeks she added, "and he's very lucky to have me!" And we'd both laugh at the truth of all her words.

They were visiting the United States from their home in Montevideo, Uruguay, and seeing me was their last stop before heading back home and then moving to Israel to retire. "This is one of the most beautiful places I've seen," he told me as soon as they drove onto the campus, "will you walk around and show me your favorite spots?" While my grandmother took a nap in my room, Lieberson and I traipsed up and down the almost 300 acres of slowly goldening late September.

"What are they singing there?" he asked as we passed the chapel where the choir was rehearsing. "That's our school's hymn, 'Jerusalem,'" I explained just as the lines, "And did those feet in ancient time, Walk upon England's mountains green" wafted through the open windows toward us. Lieberson sighed, "It's so beautiful."

"Yes," I agreed. "A beautiful hymn."

"No, not just the music," he continued, "everything here. All of you girls gathered here learning art and history and math and science and . . ." He swept his arms out . . . "life. Show me more, please."

And so we walked on and found ourselves at Roundtop, looking at the valley below and the mountains in the distance. "A lot of us come up here to look out and sit and talk. It's just breathtakingly lovely some days," I explained as we sat on the ground to take a rest. "If you look out that way you can see where three states all come together—Massachusetts, Vermont, and New Hampshire."

"And you, what do you think about when you come here?" he asked, his kind, bespectacled eyes studying my face. With a rush of tumbling words I told him how we had been studying modern European history and both World Wars. And how the atrocities and hatreds seemed to never abate. How the anger was so pointless and cruel and how people could be so unwaveringly prejudiced and petty. "And I've been thinking, lately, with all the horrors that have happened to so many, why was I able to be born? I mean, even in our family so many died in the wars, and why then was I meant to be here? It seems like I don't deserve it." I had not expected to say all of this, but he seemed to take it all in, listening and nodding as I spoke.

Then, quietly, he asked a confusing question: "Tell me—is someone buried here? I see gravestones. Who are they for?"

"The founder of this school," I replied, still confused, "Dwight L. Moody and his wife."

"Ah, I thought so," he continued. "I read a little about this place before we came. He was a Protestant minister, no? And he began this school in 1879 for girls—both rich and poor?" I could see that Lieberson had indeed found correct information. He continued, "It seems to me he was a remarkable man. Girls in those days didn't have much chance to such education and if they were poor then there was no chance. What a visionary he was! And look, from that beginning the school grew and grew and became this. Why do you think he did this?"

I had never thought about that. "I don't know," I began, "but I do know that his father died when he was young and his family was quite poor for a long time. He had a lot of brothers and sisters and there wasn't enough food for every-one. There were a lot of sacrifices."

"Ah," Lieberson exclaimed, "so maybe because of what his life was like and what he saw, he began to understand who he was and what he could contribute. And maybe part of that was starting a small school for those with limited chances—nothing grand—nothing glamorous. Just a small school where girls from many different backgrounds could explore their own minds and hearts and souls. And it grew and now, look, here you are learning so much!"

I was beginning to see his point. He continued: "Maybe part of our purpose here on Earth is to remember the past. No one knows why some live and some die. God knows, but in our Jewish religion, He doesn't really make it clear to us." Now he chuckled, shrugged his shoulders and continued, "Religions have tried to make sense of this forever. Your hymn, 'Jerusa-lem,' makes me think of that actual place. Three religions find their holy centers there, Christianity, Islam, Judaism—like your three states that you see from this hill. We keep strug-gling and searching to find that meaning from many different angles."

"So," he continued as we stood up to head back, "your Mr. Moody took what was in his history—all the pain and joy and fear and wonder and he found ways to rewrite it in his present. And then it became the past and it also became the future—the one you are in right now standing here on his grave."

I could see what he was trying to say to me, although it would take me years to fully understand.

We kept a companionable silence on our short walk to my dorm—each of us engrossed in our own thoughts. The air filled with the rustling sounds of early falling leaves gently falling on the browning grass. Suddenly I stopped and turned to him, "Lieberson, I just realized something—In the 'Jerusalem' hymn the writer of the lyrics—poet William Blake—tells us that if we want to have changes, we need to do what work we can to make it happen. And we need to remember the past to change the future. And we can start anywhere to help the world—and do it any time."

He smiled and hugged me and said: "From wherever I am in this great universe, I will be cheering you on." Suddenly we both saw my now rested and buoyant grandmother come happily toward us in the late golden light. As the chapel bells tolled the hour, and the three of us entwined our arms and walked down the path toward the waiting car, I could feel the roots of my life slowly growing downward toward the nourishing past as my limbs grew strong and reached upward toward the beckoning and mysterious future.

CHAPTER 31

BUSINESS SCHOOL

"Hey, Teresa, get over here. There's a kid blubbering all over my clean counter. She ordered an egg cream and didn't touch it. Get over here," the owner yelled to the back of the store.

It was June 1966, I was sixteen years old and in the Jamaica section of Queens, New York City. I had wandered into the corner candy store, Mazello's, underneath the gloomy elevated train tracks, on my way home from Brown's Business School.

"What's a matter which you?" she said in the distinctive regional accent I had come to recognize, as I sobbed into my hands, my body causing the already shaky tall red swivel stool to quiver. I looked up to see a girl about my age with kind brown eyes, a massive beehive hairdo, and a torn dishtowel in her hand. "You hurt or somethin'?" she continued, "'Cause you look fine. Whatcha doin' in here anyway? You look like you're dressed to go to like a polo match with a prince or sumthin'," she chuckled good naturedly as she pointed toward my shiny loafers, matching sweater set, Villager blue and white printed skirt, and carefully bobbing pony tail. She was right. I was a stark contrast to the tight-skirted, high-heeled, make-up clad, teased-haired girls in the neighborhood.

"I'm miserable." I began, "a total failure at typing. Everybody else just seems to get it fast and I . . . I just can't do it."

It was true. My father had insisted that I take a one-month course at the school because he wanted me to "be prepared for the real world." He explained it yet again four days ago before my first day of typing class. "Look, Sylvia, you're a very smart girl. You know three languages. You're going to an excellent prep school in Massachusetts, and no doubt you'll graduate from a good college. But then what? When you apply for jobs the first thing they'll want to know is how fast you can type. You need to be realistic. Women simply don't have as many choices." My general response—that I loved reading and poetry and that I wanted to be a teacher—fell on deaf ears. "This is not a punishment, my daughter. I want you to be as prepared as possible." I grudgingly agreed. After all, it was just a month, and then we'd be off to our summer home in Cape May.

I took two different busses to get from our apartment to the school and when I entered the typing center all I could see were rows upon rows upon rows of old, black Smith Corona manual typewriters. I took a seat in the back and stared down at my hands, wondering what they would do. I had prepared myself by reading books about the history of typing and the advent of printing which then led me to research a biography of Gutenberg and the first real printed edition of the Bible which then led me to a history of different publication methods.

I could see immediately that none of that would help me here.

Everyone else in the class seemed to pick up the information quickly and soon the clattering of the keys began. A white piece of paper covered the letters so we had to look up to see a large copy of the keyboard placed in front of us. I was slow. I was miserably slow. We worked steadily for two hours—the clattering and pinging ("Make sure to push the lever to go to the next line at the end of the row," the teacher reminded us as we continued) and the whirling of carriages adjusting new sheets of paper to the right position—surrounding me.

After a short break we were at it again. By the third day I was getting exasperated. Everyone was advancing but I simply could not do this. "Stop reading words," the teacher would tell me over and over and over. "Look, you see Clara and Margie over here," she pointed to my left and my right, "they don't see words when they copy. They're just seeing letters and spaces and punctuation. That's how they go fast. That's what you need to be successful here. Stop reading words. You aren't here to find meaning in these exercises. You're just here to learn how to copy." But I couldn't. And I was failing.

And so I found myself at the corner candy store in this unfamiliar neighborhood, unable to carry my mounting misery as far as the bus stop. New York City candy stores in 1966 were havens of comfort, filled with a jumble of necessities and delights for everyone. They were often rough places with torn-up floors and uneven shelves, but when there was a soda fountain, the counters were shiny and the flavors were delicious. Egg creams (ironically a soda with no eggs or cream) with Fox's U-Bet Chocolate Syrup was my favorite. But today I dissolved into a sea of frustration, unable to drink anything.

Teresa listened as I spouted my litany of failure. And she offered a suggestion. "So maybe practice doin' it backwards at first. Like start at the end of the sentence and look backwards. It'll make no sense then. Seems to me you're tryin' real hard to make sense of them phrases." She stopped and looked at her dishrag and then continued, "And sometimes ya just can't make no sense or it'll keep you from living." I brightened up. Teresa had an idea that might work. I quickly finished my soda and headed home.

The next day was better. I started off practicing the way my new friend suggested and it began to help. After class I couldn't wait to stop and tell her. "So whatcha havin' today, kid?" Mr. Mazello said to me, "I see you ain't blubberin' now." We both laughed.

"Teresa really helped me yesterday. I can't wait to tell her. Is she here?"

He yelled to the back for her and then looked at me, "I'm real proud of her. She's my oldest. When my wife died three years ago I was a broken man. I was real bad. Teresa—she just took over. I got four little ones and she just stopped goin' to school to look after everyone. And the store." He looked around proudly. "She helped me bring in new things and stack them just right."

"Papa, are you boring the princess over here," Teresa was heading toward us as she playfully teased him. He went to the back and Teresa and I started talking. I told her how much she helped me. "You know," she began, "sometimes you just gotta look at things different. Whatcha got in your hands there?" She motioned toward the book I was carrying. "Oh I'm re-reading *Jane Eyre* on the bus. I got a long ride home." She wanted to know what the book was about, so I described how Jane was orphaned and all about her trials and tribulations and how she managed and ultimately triumphed.

Teresa sighed, "I used to love reading all them books at school. So where'd ya get it at?" she asked.

"Library," I told her. She fidgeted and looked down and said, "Wish I was brave enough to go. There's one right down the block here. I always feel too stupid—don't know where to even start to look. I went in once and just got so scared I ran out."

I could see even talking about it brought terror to her eyes. "Listen," I began, "tomorrow after my classes we can go there together. I'll show you how to do it."

The following day after school I met Teresa at the candy store and walked with her to the library. We wandered around at first, just looking at row after row after row of books. "Just get the feel of it at first. Don't think about what you want yet. Just get comfortable with the whole place," I told her. I helped her get a card. She was very quiet and shy until we got outside. Then she brandished the new library card over her head, twirled around, and yelled, "My key to the world," as people passed around us. We both laughed and waved wildly as she turned left and I right to head home.

For the next few weeks I stopped every day for a soda (I had now ventured to a Black and White—chocolate syrup with vanilla ice cream) which Mr. Mazello made special for me with an extra scoop. Teresa and I checked on each other's progress. "I got five books yesterday and guess what? I took seven-year-old Maria and showed her how to find books and she got three of her own! She told me it was the most beautiful place she's ever seen," Teresa told me, "and I started reading poetry. Robert Frost is wonderful. I can almost feel the snow on my face from one of them poems."

Sadly, while I was making some progress as a typist I still was slow. So slow, in fact, that all the thirty-nine others had moved onto the stenography room and I was left alone trying to pass my test yet again. "What kind of test you gotta take?" Teresa wanted to know.

I told her, "I have to type faster than 60 words a minute to pass—with no mistakes. I can type really fast, but I always make mistakes and that gets deducted."

"So, you afraid of making mistakes?" she asked. I thought about this while twisting my straw and responded, "Maybe I am. I just feel so stupid in there—so incapable."

She nodded and said, "So stop feeling stupid. You just have to forget about how you worry. That's probably slowin' you down."

On my last day at Brown's I passed my test. Seventy-two words per minute! All of the teachers were relieved as they signed my certificate. I raced to Mazello's store to show off my achievement. Mr. M. made me the biggest sundae I'd ever seen, and Teresa handed me an envelope. "I made this special for you." I smiled and put it in my bag. She continued excitedly, "And guess what? Papa said he arranged with the high school to let me enroll in their night classes for adults. I can go there right after work. He's going to close at 7 so he can take care of the kids."

Mr. Mazello beamed. "She's such a smart girl. I want her to have all the chances in the world. I want her to be prepared for life." Teresa and I hugged each other.

"Thank you for all your help," we both said almost at the same time and broke into laughter.

"Dad, Dad, I passed," I yelled as I burst into our apartment. "Look. Seventy-two words per minute!" He smiled with pride, "Well you took on something that was very hard for you and you did it. Congratulations."

I admitted to him that this was a skill I might need to use in the future. He laughed when I continued, "Because you know, Dad, great writers use typewriters. And once the electric kind gets more popular I'll be able to go really fast."

I skipped into my room and while I smelled the dinner my mom was making, I opened Teresa's card. It said, "Thank you for helping me see the whole world. I will never forget you for teaching me how to reach out to touch ideas in books. My whole life opens up when I open the pages."

"Dr. Baer," a student recently asked, "you could have done so many other things in life, why are you a literature teacher?" I answered the same way I have for more than 50 years to that very question: "I can think of nothing more meaningful or important or rewarding to do with my life than to help open the entire universe for my students to explore."

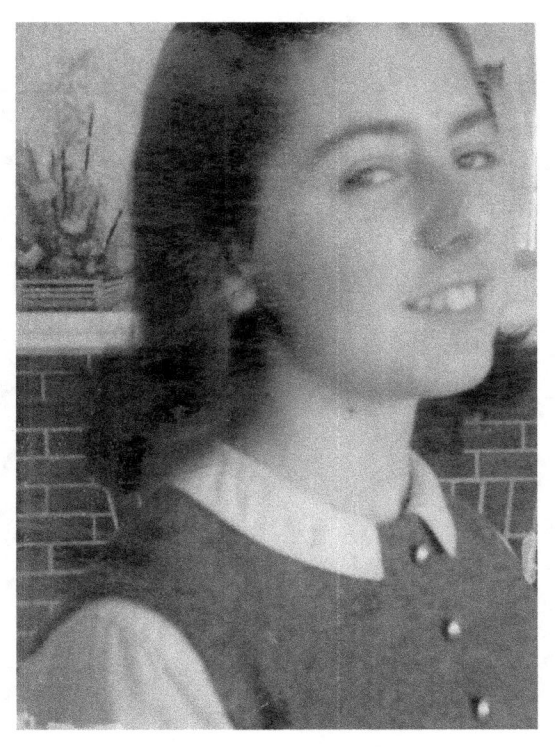

CHAPTER 32

SUCCESS

"I want you to think very carefully about this assignment. It's due on Friday." It was the first week of school, 1966, and I was a high school senior at a girls' boarding school in New England. Our institution prided itself in graduating girls who were well prepared academically for the next chapter of their lives and thus was quite rigorous in its standards and requirements. I loved everything about being there: the dorms, the traditions, the focus on books and ideas. And despite a rocky start, I did well—not a stellar student—but adequate. This was true of much of my education history.

My problem, it seemed, was that if a particular assignment or idea intrigued or inspired me, I would create something quite different from the requirements. Some teachers really liked this, and some found it, well, disturbing. No one questioned my skills—it was my adherence to the expected product that was the trouble. I figured out a coping strategy at an early age—after Mrs. Triste in the third grade sent me to the principal's office for creating a map of the world upside down. "If we float in space like a round ball, there's no up or down, is there? So why can't Africa be at the top of the map?" I reasoned.

"Because that is not the true nature of things and the sooner you learn that the better!" a red-faced Mrs. Triste yelled, pointing to the door.

I was sent to a "thinking spot" in the library by my kindly principal and came up with what turned out to be a very useful strategy. I would create two responses to interesting assignments: one that I assumed the teacher wanted and one that I took in a different direction. There were only a few teachers I would show my second version to, learning early on who was likely to be receptive. I wasn't always right. My sophomore geometry teacher did not take kindly to a set of axioms and proofs I created using only words from Shakespeare. But my fractal geometry professor (many years later) in a Yale course I audited loved my non-numerical, word-based (but not perfect) fractals.

And so it was that when my new English teacher asked us to write what we really thought, I was skeptical. My hand went up: "Miss O'Donell, is there something you want us to be sure to include? Is there actually a right answer?" She assured us there was not. The only requirement was that we be honest with ourselves and our ideas. I believed her.

Many decades later, clearing out my attic a few weeks ago, I found that very assignment and I've copied it below with its errors and quirks:

Assignment: A big theme in American literature is the concept of success. Before we begin our readings, I'd like to know what you think success is. Explain in a paragraph.

My Answer: "I think my idea of success might be different from what you're looking for. It's not about power or money or a title, or even getting high grades—I think it's bigger than that. We can think of DNA as successful because it seems to last forever because our genes are transferred from one generation to another. But to me that seems almost trivial. Yes, I do have some mannerisms like my mother, and I do have my grandmother's smile. But that seems small compared to bigger, more important things. My father is not my genetic father, but I share much more significant things with him. He taught me about perseverance. I've watched him create and lose businesses only to start another and another and never, ever lose his sense of hope. I happened upon janitors cleaning up after classes and heard them whistling or singing while doing their necessary but repetitive jobs, and I learned the power of dignity in all work. I watched my Holocaust survivor neighbor's callous, arthritic hands sew a tiny baby dress for her new grand-daughter, and I learned resilience. You see, I think that when we watch others and learn from them, we take a little part of them into our own beings. And when we do things for others—no matter how small—part of us goes into them. And that changes them and when they do something, part of me gets passed along. So, I need to be very careful that what I pass along to the world—what will live forever—are the things that make the world better. If this happens, I will be a success."

"Sylvia," she wrote at the top, "this paragraph has made me re-think some ideas I hold. It will change a part of me. You are already on the road to success."

Miss O'Donell, long gone from the Earth, still lives in me, and still I strive for the same kind of success I envisioned as a sixteen-year-old.

EMILY DICKINSON: 749

All but Death, can be Adjusted—
Dynasties repaired—
Systems—settled in their Sockets—
Citadels—dissolved—

Wastes of Lives—resown with Colors
By Succeeding Springs—
Death—unto itself—Exception—
Is exempt from Change—

CHAPTER 33

OCEAN DECK

"I see that Joe Sr. is over at your station tonight," Penny said. It was July 1968, I was eighteen years old and working a double shift waitressing at the Ocean Deck Restaurant, exactly six blocks from my family's summer cottage. The Deck was the kind of place that sits right on the beach, and you barely needed to put on shoes and a bathing suit cover-up to eat there. It was busy and crowded and noisy. I normally loved this job, but today seemed unusually long and my normally crisp white uniform was stained where some coffee had splattered and where a leftover piece of blueberry pie had slid, lava-like, off my tray and onto my lap while I was clearing Table 7. Penny was the most talkative one of the staff and since she lived in town all year, she had stories about everyone who wasn't a tourist.

"You know," she continued, "he just hasn't ever been right since his wife died in that car crash last fall. And then just a few months later when Joe Jr. went and killed himself—well, he's a wreck. Just look at him." I pushed the red button on the coffee maker to start a new pot and while I waited to make sure I heard the plopping sound of the water hitting the ground beans, I glanced over at him. He was at the table near the sand and water. Sitting there, even amidst all the noise and color of the restaurant, he looked isolated—like a granite island perched almost tentatively on the rickety, weathered chair. He had been coming in almost daily for dinner, which he ordered, but never finished. He was never rude, but just didn't engage anyone in conversation. He seemed to be getting thinner before our eyes. Penny continued, "Nobody's seen him cry or even get upset. My mom says that he goes to work every day at the county office, but he don't talk to nobody. Just does his work and leaves." And then she said, "Whoops, you got another table. A family it looks like. Don't recognize them. Uh-oh. Monica put them right next to Joe Sr." I grabbed some slightly grimy plastic-coated menus, walked to their table, and greeted them.

There were four in the family: The mother and a young boy of about ten sat down first, and the father pulled a chair out, very ceremoniously, for a little girl with dark brown springy curls. She giggled as I approached. "Hi," she said looking up at me, "My name's Mirabella, and it's my birthday I'm six today and this is my very first time ever in a fancy restaurant and look what mommy and daddy gave me." As she started fishing around in her pockets I noticed the soft, kind faces of the two parents, and the father's calloused and rough hands leaning gently on the table. She took out a coin. "Look. A really shiny quarter! Daddy said I can spend it on anything I want but I never had so much money before and I don't know what I want to get."

"Mirabella," her mother admonished her, "this nice young lady is our waitress and she wants to know what you want to eat for your special dinner."

"I've been dreaming about this for days," Mirabella began, "and I know exactly: a cheeseburger and fries and a chocolate milkshake please. And see my new dress?" I smiled as she pointed to it and she continued, "Mommy got it special for me for tonight. It's almost like new—probably only been worn by a couple of girls a few times. Isn't it just beautiful?"

Now I noticed the mother's ill-fitting and faded dress, the holes in the sagging sweater the father was wearing, and the too tight but perfectly ironed shirt the young boy had on. Penny walked by balancing a massive tray and the boy followed the food with his eyes. I spoke, "Well, the birthday girl has ordered a delicious dinner. What can I get for the rest of you?"

The father quickly answered, "Just water please. We're not very hungry." The boy looked down.

I knew what was happening. I didn't know, however, that Joe Sr. had been watching and listening. As I was getting ready to move away from the table, he leaned over and said to the family, "I'm here by myself tonight. And I got these coupons for five free meals. I only used one and they expire today. Would you folks like the others? I'd hate to see them go to waste."

And then he looked me square in the eyes and I knew to follow along. The young boy's face lit up. The father spoke, "Well, that's mighty kind of you . . .".

"Not kind at all," said Joe Sr. "I just don't want them to not get used. I'll just go give them to the manager. Order anything you like."

An excited family grabbed the menus and began discussing as I followed Joe Sr. to the cash register. He pulled out his wallet and handed me fifty dollars. "Look," he said, "I don't ever want them to know there were no coupons. I just want them to have a memorable dinner. If it's more than this, I'll pay more tomorrow." And right before heading back to his table he said, "Nothing is more important than being with people you love."

I was taken aback, but delighted by this, and with an extra spring in my step, went back to Mirabella and her family. They gleefully ordered modest dinners with milkshakes all around. Joe Sr. sat quietly at his table nearby, sipping his coffee and looking out at the water. After dinner, the birthday girl asked me a question, "I want to buy a piece of cake all by myself. Not a coupon," and she pulled out her quarter. "Is this enough money?" I assured her it was, but I looked at her parents. "Yes, it's fine. It's her present to do as she pleases," her mother told me. "I'd like the chocolatiest chocolate cake please," she giggled as she presented me with her coin. I came back a few minutes later with the dessert, as the family was gathering their things to leave. They had just finished thanking Joe Sr. again for the coupons and were talking and laughing happily.

I was confused, but Mirabella took the cake from my hands and walked over to Joe Sr. She set it down in front of his slumped and thin frame. "I just wanted to give you something because you looked so sad. You're such a nice man and I'll never forget my magical birthday where I went to a real restaurant and my whole family got to eat dinner. All of us!" She patted his shoulder with her little hand and skipped away following her parents and brother out the door.

When I went over to top off Joe Sr.'s coffee, he looked over at the now-empty table—then looked out at the water. And, for the first time, I saw him smile—seemingly at the sky, the ocean, a passing seagull. He turned to me, eyes brimming with tears, and said, "It really still is a beautiful world, isn't it?"

CHAPTER 34

AMPUTATION

"Amputation is the only recourse we have. The surgery is underway now," my father told me over the phone. It was June 1970, the summer before my senior year of college. My mother and I had been shopping for fabrics at a store near our small New Jersey town. She and I wandered up and down the aisles looking at bolt after bolt of glorious fabric. Taffetas, silks, organzas, cottons, wools—we both loved to run our hands over the material and feel the uniqueness of each weave. I was determined to sew some new skirts and dresses for all the events planned for my final year of college. "I'll need this for our fall formal—I can make it into a great dress with a high waist and balloon sleeves," I gushed, holding a pink crinkled fabric blend in my arms. "I'd like five yards of this please. And three of this one. And this is just for around the collar, so one yard will be fine," I pointed and motioned to the lady behind the counter who was armed with thick glasses dangling around her neck on a beaded chain, a large pair of scissors in her right hand, and a long ruler. She cut the required amounts, we paid for our goods, and loaded down with fabrics—oh the clothing possibilities!—we left the store.

Chattering and laughing, we walked on the sidewalk heading home. At that moment, a distracted driver swerved his car onto the sidewalk, pinning my mother and me, like two bug specimens, against the brick wall of the building behind us. There was much confusion as he just kept ramming and ramming the car into us, unable to distinguish forward from reverse. He finally stopped, and alerted by our screams, helpers raced out from offices and buildings, calling for ambulances, trying to stop the bleeding, holding us steady.

We both suffered many injuries. I had multiple casts on my legs, swollen and damaged arms and back, and I was bedridden for several months with some organ damage.

"You will be fine. You'll heal. But the internal scars are deep and dangerous," they told me. My mother suffered most of all. She hovered between life and death for more than a week. When gangrene set in, her leg had to be amputated to save her life. My father called from the hospital to tell me. I was frozen—unable to speak, and unable to move from the pain and from the plaster that surrounded my shattered limbs.

Over the next few months while I healed slowly at home, my mother went from one hospital to the next—recovering in stages from the physical trauma, and being fitted with one prosthesis after another to help her regain some mobility. By late August she was home, and I had been cut out of my casts and had begun to heal well. At the insistence of my parents, I went back to my college where everything, including the walk up three floors to my dorm room, became a challenge.

I threw myself into my schoolwork and into the social whirl around me, but I found it almost impossible. My legs and body were strong now and few visible scars remained, but I was losing focus in my studies. By second semester I was struggling to maintain emotional and mental balance. Things that had seemed shiny with importance now seemed dull and rusted. I went to parties and events with my patient friends and caring boyfriend and tried to find a measure of fun. But everything was difficult.

Toward the end of second semester, the professor of my last required English course, Modern American Literature, found my lack of focus distasteful. "I am very sorry to see you go so much downhill, Sylvia. You did show some promise early on, but I must have been mistaken. Your work seems, well, undisciplined," he said during a short conference. His brow was furled into deep wrinkles between his eyes, and his mouth and nose looked as if he'd smelled something rather putrid. He continued, "I'm afraid that going into a master's program is not for you. It's just as well," he finished, standing from his high-back wooden chair and dismissing me quickly, "You haven't really learned much and, as a woman, you don't have much to offer in the world of literature." He slammed his office door behind me.

In truth my work was not up to my own standards. But later that night his words echoed like the banging door in that old brick English department building, pounding—it seemed—at the scars on my legs, my arms, my mind. And the anger and frustration and fear of the past year seemed to well up inside my chest—a balloon filled too full—too ready to burst at any minute.

I drove the three hours back to my home for the weekend. And while my parents were busily trying to sell our three-story home and move to a more practical—more manageable for my mom—one-level house, I began two projects of my own. "Why are you up here in the attic? It's after midnight. What are you doing?" my father called up to me as he ascended the creaky steps. "Oh, I see," he said, kissed the top of my head and left. I was at my sewing machine, having found those bags of fabric from last summer that had somehow gotten shoved into a dark corner under the eaves. The parts that were blood-stained—rust-colored now—I cut away. I still had enough for a pink skirt and a white top. I sewed much of the night and into the next day. Exhausted, I drove back to campus.

Days later I wrote my final English paper with renewed enthusiasm and reimagined focus. My professor was not impressed. I had chosen what he considered to be a minor Hemingway novel, *The Old Man and the Sea*. And he called my focus, "awkward." But I realized that while he was a scholar in his field, perhaps I had been too narrow in my own thinking. And now I began to feel that I had begun to cast off all manner of constraints. I had learned a great deal, but it was time to determine how I would fashion my life. And I chose.

That paper and that novel is all that I truly remember from the foggy haze that surrounded my schoolwork that year. And I carry the memory to this day. In the book, the main character, Santiago, a poor, old fisherman by trade, tries, one last time, to catch the giant fish which has eluded him his whole life. As we read on we watch his struggles form into a bond of understanding between man and fish. Nonetheless, struggles they are. In the end he catches it, but in transporting the fish boat-side in the water toward his home, fate takes an unexpected turn and sharks eat it. However, this was and is a story of triumph not tragedy. Santiago battled the fear and pain and isolation within himself and ultimately he overcame it. The fish was not the prize. His transcendence was.

That June, under my formal robes for my graduation I wore my self-made skirt and top. And my mother, balancing on her crutches and beaming with pride, took my picture.

CHAPTER 35

Just a Boy
(OR, THREADS)

"He was only a boy—seventeen, maybe eighteen years old." It was 1973, I was twenty-three years old, and my grandmother was visiting me in my brand-new home in Maryland. I was recovering from emergency surgery and she had come for a week to keep me company. We sat in my living room that day—I wistfully looking out at the bright day and trying not to think about the pain or the scars on my abdomen, and she sewing a hem on one of my dresses.

Uncharacteristically, she started talking about Poland. "Yes, he was just a boy. I was about your age, and very pregnant with your uncle Max. Your mother was just three years old then, and I was too tired and overwhelmed to take the usual precautions," she continued. Ah. The "precautions." A while back she had told me tales about the Polish pogroms where soldiers ransacked Jewish homes, often killing or maiming the families. At her family's home there was a trap door under an old rug under the kitchen table where sometimes she and (later) the two children had to hide until the sounds of the men's boots and horses disappeared—sometimes minutes, often hours.

But this time, she was alone with my mother and was too big and awkward to hide. "When he burst in through the door, I could see right away that he was scared. He was so young. I heard the commander order him from the road to take anything they could sell. The boy's eyes moved quickly over the room. There was almost nothing there. Then he saw the silver candle stick on the cabinet and went to grab it. Your mother (such a small sickly little girl) ran to stop him, but I pulled her back. He looked at us. 'I have to take this. They will hurt my family if I don't obey them. I have to do it.'"

"So what did you do?" I asked my grandmother. "Did you say anything to make him leave it alone? What did you do?"

She answered, "I did the only thing that was right for me to do: I told him there was some tea in a pot on the stove. I knew he was thirsty and hungry. We had no food but there was tea. And I told him to please drink it. He was welcome to take the old candlestick—it would save him and his family."

I stared at her in astonishment. "What? He was robbing you. He was part of the group that was hurting people. How could you offer him tea?"

She looked at me calmly. "Sylvia, he was a boy. He was afraid. I was afraid. I knew how it felt. He had to do what he had to do to save himself and his family. The only power I had at that moment was the power of compassion—he was thirsty and I had tea."

I took a deep breath and asked, "What happened next?" She continued, "Well, we lived there for three or four more years. We had scares but had nothing left for anyone to steal, and we would always hide. But when things were getting worse and worse, beatings, killings, I knew I had to find a way out of the country—find a way to safety for me and the two children. Jews could not get papers to travel. It was forbidden, so I had to find a way to get some forged documents. I did it and we set off.

"There was only one checkpoint I was really afraid of. It was near our village and someone might recognize us. We all three walked to the guards. A young local officer approached us and my knees almost went weak with fear and then with recognition. He asked for our papers, looked at me, smiled, and stamped them for travel approval. Very quietly he leaned down and said, 'Thank you for the tea. It was the best I will ever taste.'" I could only stare at my grandmother calmly stitching.

"So, it was him? Him?" I said in astonishment. "Yes." She nodded toward me. "You see, Sylvia," she continued, "even when the whole world is in chaos, when life seems out of their control, most people are good and want to help." She smiled at me and I could see that her old eyes were tired.

"Here it is," she said as she cut the last bit of thread. "It's all finished now."

EMILY DICKINSON: 508

I'm ceded—I've stopped being Theirs—
The name They dropped upon my face
With water, in the country church
Is finished using, now,
And They can put it with my Dolls,
My childhood, and the string of spools,
I've finished threading—too—

Baptized, before, without the choice,
But this time, consciously, of Grace—
Unto supremest name—
Called to my Full—The Crescent dropped—
Existence's whole Arc, filled up,
With one small Diadem.

My second Rank—too small the first—
Crowned—Crowing—on my Father's breast—
A half unconscious Queen—
But this time—Adequate—Erect,
With Will to choose, or to reject,
And I choose, just a Crown—

CHAPTER 36

La Sociedad

"La sociedad de mujeres intelectuales y brillantes," she told me in Spanish. I translated quickly in my head—"The society of intellectual and brilliant women." Aha. I smiled as I looked at the picture she put in front of us on the table. It was 1974, I was twenty-four years old, and my grandmother was visiting me for a week. She had come from across the ocean to my home in Maryland. I was embarking on my adult life having just gotten married, bought a home, started my teaching career, and begun my (first) master's degree.

Spanish was the language we communicated in, but it was her fifth language. As a young girl in Lomza, Poland, she spoke Polish, German, and Russian. She told me, "We never knew which language we might need. First one army invaded, then another. We learned to listen and speak what they were speaking. It kept us safer." "French, too. Yes. I learned the language of fashion and hats when I was young. Oh, that was a musical language." After she emigrated to Uruguay, in 1930, she quickly learned the native language, Spanish. "You know," she said, "my name in Polish is Malka, but when I started my women's hat-making shop in Montevideo, I changed my name to Margot. So much lovelier a sound. I love the sound of words," and she sighed happily as she sipped her Earl Gray out of my new Wedgewood teacup—the Volendam pattern, with a singing bird on a branch by its nest poised to take flight.

She had brought some essentials for our visit: good sewing needles of various sizes, a collection of very old buttons, and some photographs. Today she showed me a picture, from 1916, of a gathering of young women. "You see, women were not thought to have very much in the way of brains for higher thought. Ha! How small-minded those men were. We didn't have access to libraries or lectures. But some of us were determined to hear the big ideas of the world. Our town was so small (on the far northeastern border of Russia), but our minds—they were big and they were hungry. We girls got together to talk. Our fathers thought we were discussing food or sewing, but some of our mothers knew the truth. Do you see her?" she said pointing to the girl in the far left chair, "her father was a doctor. When her mother cleaned his library bookshelves she would take out books—one a time so as not to create suspicion—and leave them on the floor near the door. Annika—who was prohibited from setting foot in that room—would walk by, put the book under her skirt and bring it to our meetings. One time Greta—the girl with the tie, standing up—paid a young peasant boy to go into the library and steal a book (a Martin Buber book!) because we were so desperate to read those ideas." She paused to nibble on the chocolate chip cookies I had baked that morning.

I knew that when she was a girl, my grandmother's father wouldn't let her go to the university, and that she made money modeling hats in fine stores which she used to pay her way so she could secretly earn a degree as a pharmacist. ("No one knew I was a Jew. They would not have allowed me in. Bad enough I was a woman!") But I had never heard of her life before that. "You know, Abuela," I said to her as the sun shone through the big picture window of my living room, "even now in 1974 they tell me that women should not worry about getting higher degrees—being doctors or lawyers or philosophers or college professors. When I graduated from high school the best universities didn't allow women to enter. Even now it's such a small number." I slumped lower into the couch beside her.

"Look at this picture," she said almost violently pointing. "Look. You see these girls? We got together. We found a way. We began. See Elza there?" she said pointing to the girl with her chin resting on her hand. "She learned Morse code and helped get Jews out of our town in 1935 by tapping on walls and floors. She lives in Israel today and works as a translator. And Ada, sitting with her hand on her temple, she dressed as a German soldier in 1939 and led twenty-five children to safety. Then she became an artist." She smiled and looked at the picture again. "And that's me," she said pointing to the slim girl on the far right leaning on the cabinet. "I'm going to be the first one of this group with a granddaughter who will get a doctorate degree." I laughed and said, "Abuela, I'm only just beginning a master's degree. I don't know if I can go that far." She put down her cup, grabbed me by the shoulder and looked me squarely in the eye. "Yes you will. Women have their own, personal, individual stars inside of them and we find a way—we find a way—to shine brilliantly."

Thirteen years later, eleven years after she died, I framed my newly earned degree in gold.

CHAPTER 37

TRADITIONS

"Benny, you're exaggerating," my father called out laughing. It was late August 1970, I was getting ready to start my senior year of college, and two of his college buddies had come to visit us at our summer house for their annual BBQ Extravaganza Weekend, which they'd started a few years back. Benny, an Episcopal priest; Manny, a rabbi; and my father, a businessman, would spend two days eating, drinking, telling stories, and laughing so hard that the house seemed to shake with hilarity.

"No, it's the absolute truth, Sylvia," Benny continued, "Fred, your father, saw that everyone left the stands at the halftime shows of our Hamilton College football games. He knew he had to do something."

Manny now jumped in, "Because he was the bandleader, he felt responsible for a good show. So you know what he did?

He took the three-hour train ride down to New York City and somehow arranged for chorus girls to perform as part of our show the following week."

Now Manny's laughter was so intense that Benny had to continue, "You know, Hamilton is an all-male college, and it was not seen as appropriate for women to participate at football games. And, he did ask for permission from the administrators. And what did they say, Fred?" he called to my dad, who had started up the grill in the yard.

My father responded, "They said 'absolutely not.' They said it was 'against all traditions' to have women perform. I pleaded with them, and then tried to reason with them that with a better show more people would attend. It had gotten too stogy. Too fuddy-duddy. Too out-of-date."

"What happened?" I asked trying to quell their laughter for the rest of the story. "What happened?"

"Well," Manny continued, "Turned out that the November 15, 1947, show was a huge success. Fred was going to be in big trouble, but the alumni at the game loved it. They thought it added a much-needed freshness and fun, and they praised the bandleader for having the ingenuity to do this."

Now my dad jumped in, "I even got a very unusual pat on the back from the college president."

"Traditions are a strange thing, aren't they?" I mused aloud. I was very conflicted about this topic. "Seems to me that a true tradition never would change, but they always do." I had been mourning the fact that the girls' prep school I had attended for four years was soon to become co-ed. "All of those traditions we had will be gone. It does make me sad," I sighed.

"But look," Benny began, "people change, needs change, the world is constantly changing. Even in our church we've adapted so much. Soon we'll even have women ministers. And why not? I mean, things need to change to stay alive."

Manny now chimed in, "Probably next year there will be women rabbis, and there are many changes to our rituals as well."

My father now smiled, "And I hear tell that Yale is now admitting women." He knew this was a sore spot for me.

I responded forcefully, "Having Ivy League colleges be 'traditionally all-male' is totally antediluvian (a term I had learned recently and used over and over). The best educational institutions should be open for all to compete equally."

Now they all laughed uproariously. "Fred, your daughter is following your tradition of up-ending tradition, isn't she?"

I joined in, but continued, "It's so confusing, though. What good are traditions anyway? They don't last. And yet, I do find comfort in them." Manny smiled, "Sylvia, traditions should never be confused with what they stand for."

Benny continued, "Churches can burn down, institutions change scholars, people die—life changes. What lasts are the things that remind us that we are all part of something bigger than ourselves—that yes, we exist as individuals, but we are all part of something grander. And, ultimately, knowing you are part of the immensity of the human family and of the universe, and feeling in your own heart that others' hearts are also beating and that far into the future hearts will beat—in different worlds, but the same human hearts—that's the whole point. The acts change, but the meaning remains the same: We are in this world together."

My father announced the food was ready and we all sat around the table with plates piled high. Benny said one prayer, Manny said another, and we began the meal. "Why is that big bowl of apples on that front hall table," asked one of them, pointing.

"Every year when Sylvia goes back to school, I give her an apple to start off her new school-year journey. It's a tradition," my father said winking at me.

Years later, I did some post-graduate research at Yale and was made a Yale Associate Fellow (Davenport) several years ago. My beloved prep school, a combined co-ed institution since 1971, had its fiftieth reunion, which renewed old friendships and began new ones. My father's college was opened to women and my daughter—his granddaughter—graduated from there in the year 2000. Women were, indeed, able to become Jewish rabbis and Episcopal priests, and the world has changed in unimaginable ways. But still love beats our hearts. And still we are all connected in our grand universal tradition of humanity.

And still apples are on my table.

EMILY DICKINSON: 1142

The Props assist the House
Until the House is built
And then the Props withdraw
And adequate, erect,
The House support itself
And cease to recollect
The Auger and the Carpenter—
Just such a retrospect
Hath the perfected Life—
A past of Plank and Nail
And slowness—then the Scaffolds drop
Affirming it a Soul.

CHAPTER 38

TEARING DOWN

"So much destruction—I can't bear to look at it. My heart hurts," the letter said. My father's parents came to the U.S. from Germany in 1923. Transatlantic travel being much harder back then, their first trip back to their birth country for a visit was in 1938. He spoke often of the visit and the realization of what their country was becoming. "So civilized a place—great philosophers, composers, artists, scientists—now it turned to brutal ideas. A great place torn apart by hate and greed and fear."

The next visit was in 1951—a few years after the end of WWII. I was surprised to learn that my grandfather, Max, kept a meticulous journal of that journey. I read it recently, having been given a box of mementos rescued from his attic's eaves by a kind neighbor and by the demolition company tearing down my grandparents' house (after it had changed many hands).

In the writings, Max recounts the ocean voyage, the changing colors of the sea, the anticipation. And then, when in Germany, he writes of the horror and sadness of his wife's first sight of her old neighborhood. "All of downtown destroyed! Can't find way around anymore—museum damaged—destruction—ruins throughout—most houses burned out . . . Wilma too shocked to cry." He writes this not in his native language but in English. I imagined him communicating with me, his only grandchild, in a language I could later understand.

I put the journal down, so saddened by the vivid descriptions. Then, this afternoon, I got a text from a kind friend: It was a photo he took that very morning of the home my parents had lived in from the early 1970s until their deaths 30 years later. It was being bulldozed to make way for new townhouses. So much upheaval. So much destruction. How much, I thought, do we tear down in our lifetime? Not even buildings with solid foundations survive. Not human lives. Way leads on to way.

So what lasts? What can we count on in this ever-changing world? Where are humanity's struggles and joys and loves and angers and fears and sadness and transcendence? Maybe— maybe—it's all in the telling of its stories.

And in the listening.

very ... Good... Daughter. ... with ...
... he was in any hotel. Paper ...
Monday, Sep. 10th — Said goodbye to ...
relatives after breakfast with them, ...
Autobahn. Drive to Hannover. Found ...
HOTEL ZUR POST near Bahnhof. New ...
in fine this jack. Desk clerk ex — Have ...
Have nice room with shower — needed show...
felt good — Walk thru down town — very ...
all of down town destroyed! Much rebui...
shops — can't find way around anymore ...
three years — Museum damaged — Mar...
lost roof — destruction in residential ...
small people worst! Ruins remov...
burned out. People told story of bo...
first bombing with jelly oil bombs, ...
fighters killing people on streets. ...
ever forget!   Wilma called her ...
... over at 7 p.m. — Uli came — Ver...
... 80 men working — two children ...
... was bad!

CHAPTER 39

ROUGH TRANSLATION

We were having another of our marathon arguments. They were always around the same theme: expectations. I was her only child and my mother expected me to be more like her, and I expected her to understand my difference. "You could have been a real doctor," she yelled, "instead of this other kind you're studying for. Real doctors save lives. What is this PhD going to do to help your husband? Your daughter? Anyone?" It was 1987, I was 37 years old, and had just successfully finished defending my dissertation. I expected her to be proud of me. She didn't seem to be anything other than disappointed.

We were, in truth, very different. Her language was Spanish and while I started my life in that tongue, as soon as we moved to the U.S. when I was seven, I fell in love with English. At first she would ask me to translate some words or phrases but soon she had a great command of the language. She was never fully comfortable with it, though, and would revert to Spanish whenever she could. I was always a voracious reader, devouring whole library shelves in a week, whereas she read some newspapers and always the fashion sections, but never read books. She insisted on absolute neatness and "lady-like" behavior, whereas I was a messy kid more prone to excitedly riding my bike (and falling off and skinning my knee) and rumpled clothes. She loved opera, and I could not tolerate the loudness. She was frustrated by a halt in her education as a medical student, and I cared nothing about science or math. In short, we were different.

This particular argument lasted longer than the others. We both seemed more entrenched, angry, and disappointed. In my final frustration I yelled, "You don't like anything I do and you don't understand my life. I wish you valued me more." Even as I said it I knew it wasn't fully true, but I was beyond reason at that point and stormed into my childhood bedroom to cry tears of confusion.

A few minutes later my father knocked quietly at my door. He came in, sat next to me on the bed, and started talking. "I know you and your mother seem to be so different. But I want you to know she really is proud of you, and she really does appreciate your work even if she doesn't understand it." At that point he opened a piece of paper he had walked in with. "Look," he said, "this traveled with us for more than twenty years. She's kept it in her jewelry case"—a prized location!— "all this time. She reads it aloud sometimes and marvels that, as she says, 'my own daughter wrote this just for me.'" He handed me the paper on which I had written a poem in 1966, when I was sixteen and in prep school in New England. I wrote it in (not perfect) Spanish with great care for the rhyme and meter.

I was astonished. "She kept this all these years?" Suddenly I felt waves of remorse and even more confusion. "Why? She doesn't like poetry—she's told me that so many times."

He looked at me, "Sylvia, you wrote this in her language. *Her* language."

I took the poem with me to the dining room where my mother was sitting with a cup of tea looking distractedly out the window. She saw the paper in my hand and then looked into my eyes. I sat across from her and started speaking in Spanish. I asked her why she stopped her studies, what she missed about Uruguay, what color bathing suit she recommended I buy. We talked. And then we talked some more. And as I was getting up from the table, she stopped me. "You know what I loved about the poem? I loved that you told a story about the sun and the stars and traveling in the universe. And you did it just for me." And then she said, "You have a poet's soul. I have been astonished by that your whole life. You see things differently than I do, but in this poem, when you were sixteen, you wanted me to be part of your world and you wanted me to travel up the skies with you."

Now I saw it: My writing mattered to her a lot—but I had not been using a language she really understood. Understanding requires a common language and some translation.

Later that year when I was awarded my degree, a PhD in English, and officially became Dr. Kuhner-Baer, my parents had a large party for me. It was a fun time with much laughter and eating and dancing. At one point I saw my mom sitting by herself. I took two glasses of champagne over and handed one to her. She smiled, held it up toward the sky, and in English said, "I am proud of my daughter, who is now a doctor of words!"

Years later, in 2004, after her death, I found the poem once again in her jewelry box. You can see in the upper corner where she inscribed that date—I can run my fingers over her writing and almost feel her with me. When it became time for me to design a headstone for my parents' grave, I wrote this: "Travelers of the Universe Now—Bon Voyage."

(A clumsy translation), by Sylvia Kuhner Baer

The sun that illuminates the day
Falls slowly into the ocean
Of the sky, and with a grandeur, dies--
Leaving behind a stillness through the earth.

In the entering darkness
One by one the lanterns of the sky
Light up
To guide the travelers on their way.

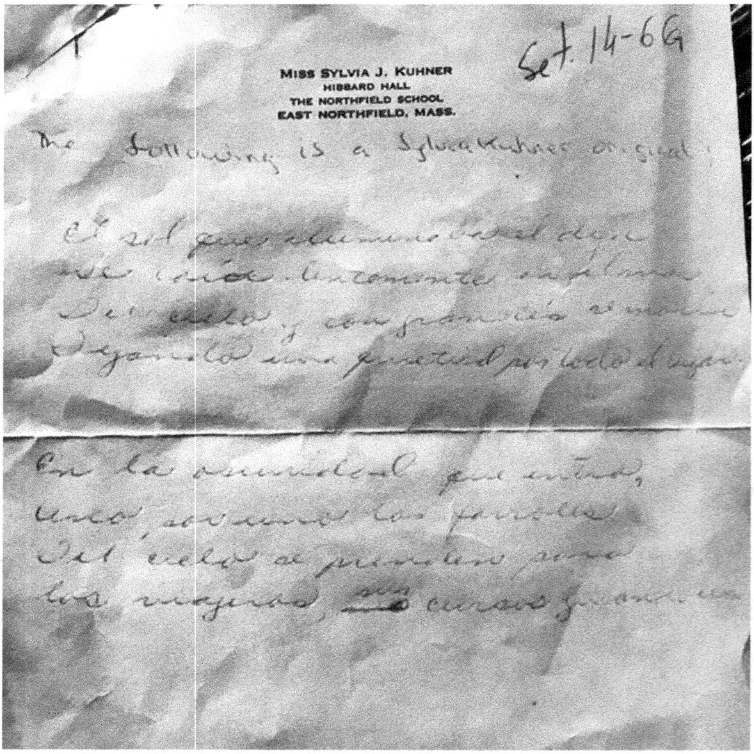

MISS SYLVIA J. KUHNER
HIBBARD HALL
THE NORTHFIELD SCHOOL
EAST NORTHFIELD, MASS.

Set. 14-66

The following is a Sylvia Kuhner original:

[handwritten Spanish text, illegible]

[handwritten Spanish text, illegible]

En la oscuridad que entra,
uno, se ama los faroles
[illegible]
los mujeres, [illegible]

IN LOVING
MEMORY
OF

FRED & SARITA
KUHNER

TRAVELERS OF THE
UNIVERSE NOW —
BON VOYAGE

CHAPTER 40

MISS KUHNER

"Miss Kuhner," she told me, "I don't see that you have the makings of a teacher."

It was fall 1970 and I was devastated. As far back as I could remember, I knew that I wanted to teach. My future was never in question. My senior year student teaching supervisor and education professor, Dr. McHugh, was delighted to place me with a very experienced teacher, Mrs. C., who I would follow throughout the day for a while, and then slowly I would take over one class for several weeks.

I sat in the back of the room and took notes as she taught remedial twelfth grade, advanced tenth grade, and intermediate ninth-grade English. I watched as she exacted responses from the students and reminded them of the daily quizzes. There was no discussion about the material. In the twelfth-grade class, I had little use initially for taking notes since the lessons were very rote and, frankly, boring. Instead, my papers were full of details about the kids in the class—all of whom were frozen in their seats. "Donna looks scared again today. She's biting her nails a lot. I wonder if she's having problems understanding." And, "Jeff keeps hitting his leg like it's falling asleep. I've noticed that he limps a lot. Maybe he needs some help." And, "Marcie has been wearing the same clothes for three days now, and she looks so tired."

About the second week I saw some of the twelfth-grade students at lunch time and I began to talk with them and offered to give them extra help if they wanted it. Several were grateful and took me up on my offer and I began to get to know them a little bit. Carol, it turned out, wrote amazing poetry so I taught her about the sonnet form to try. Jeremy, I discovered, had terrible eyesight but no money for glasses. I talked to the school counselor who directed him to an organization that would help. And when shy Sara, who was born in Cuba, discovered that my first language was Spanish, she was elated. "This means I can be something too!" she gushed.

A few days later Mrs. C. met with me after school. "You should not be helping those students," she informed me. "They need to know that they are not really high school material. They should just drop out and go get jobs."

I was stunned. "I don't understand," I said. "Shouldn't we be trying to give them the best we can so that they can be the best version of themselves?"

Her sudden piercing laugh scared me. "Have you taken a

good look at these children? They will never make anything of their lives. Now the ones in my grade ten class, they are worth helping." I was shaken. This was not really teaching. It was something else, but it was not teaching.

When it came time for me to lead a class, Mrs. C. assigned me the twelfth graders. I tried several different methods to engage the students. I told stories; I asked questions; I pointed to passages in the texts that were interesting and showed details about characters and ideas. They were not all success-ful lessons. Some were total flops. But I went back day after day determined to help them discover ideas in literature and in themselves.

And at the end of my eight-week student-teaching stint, Mrs. C. sat with my professor and me and gave me her assess-ment. "You simply don't have what it takes. You have to face it. Find something else to do." She pounded the edges of the papers she was holding on the dark oak table between us and started to pull her chair back to stand.

Dr. McHugh stopped her. "Mrs. C., can you please tell me why specifically you think this?" And she was more than happy to detail all of my "silly" attempts at engaging the stu-dents and all of my naive notions about learning abilities, and my useless waste of time trying to get "those ignorant chil-dren" to understand. Dr. McHugh then thanked her for her time and very courteously walked her to the door. They spoke in hushed tones for a minute before she left abruptly. His dark brown eyes were flashing with rage by the time he faced me across the table.

I was limp—a diminished young girl whose dreams were crumbling. I felt my entire existence to be a sort of sham. If I couldn't be the one thing I felt in the very marrow of my bones I was meant to be, then who was I?

He looked me squarely in the eyes. "You, Sylvia Kuhner," he said, "are a teacher. You always have been, you always will be. It's not what you do; it's who you are. Trust yourself. Mrs. C. has a very narrow view of the world. We will not be using her as a model again." Then his gaze went to the window for a moment and back to me. "Every single child has dignity and deserves a chance to succeed. Every single child should be honored and supported and celebrated. And I know, I know, you feel the same way." I nodded in full agreement.

For days I went over and over the events, unable to reconcile the pieces, but delighted at Dr. McHugh's assessment of my teaching potential. About a week later I talked about this with my friend Clara, a cafeteria worker at the college and a local town resident. "So who was this teacher you were workin' with?" she asked. When I told her, she laughed. "Oh, Mrs. C. Why, everybody knows about her. She only likes the rich kids—she doesn't think the rest of the kids should even be bothering with school." She yelled over to Johnny, who was sweeping up, "Hey, Sylvia here was told by Mrs. C. over at the high school that she's never gonna be a good teacher. What d'ya think about that?" Johnny chuckled, "Well, I think that makes Sylvia about the best teacher in the whole world." All three of us burst out laughing. "You know," Clara said, "you can learn a lot from people like Dr. McHugh about what you want to be like, but you can also learn who you don't want to be—like from Mrs. C. Everybody can show you something about life." I agreed.

The following September I began my first job as a teacher to my very own seventh-grade class at Lower Regional School in Cape May, New Jersey. On the first day of school, as I looked out into the sea of anxious, eager faces, I knew I was in love. There was nothing else in the world that I wanted to do—nothing else that felt so meaningful or was so much fun. As my work continued, I reveled in my students' successes and really worked to help them learn about the material, about life, and about themselves. I helped and prodded and nudged and played every single day. I loved each and every one of them.

When our class picture was taken in October there was much giggling and twisting about as the photographer and I tried to produce an orderly portrait. Finally, to create a more somber tone, I said to the class: "Imagine looking at this picture way in the future—maybe fifty years from now. You're going to be so amazed at who you were in 1971. You're getting this picture taken for the you of 2021." This worked.

Later, as we were adjusting ourselves into our normal classroom configuration, I asked them to think about their future selves and what they would be proud for having accomplished. There were all manner of responses. One girl wanted to cure cancer so no one else had to lose their mom to it like she did. One boy wanted to go into the Coast Guard like his dad and protect our coastlines. Another boy wanted to drive a giant truck all over the country. A girl wanted to be a hair-stylist and have her own salon. And then Billy asked me, "So what do *you* want to be proud of in 2021, Miss Kuhner?" My answer was immediate, "Having been caring and helpful and inspiring to years and years and years of students."

And although the formats have changed in unimaginable ways, and my age-range shifted a long time ago from seventh grade to college, I am humbled and proud to have kept the same goal for a career of more than fifty years.

ACKNOWLEDGMENTS

Thanks go to Marc J. Lane of the Law Offices of Marc J. Lane for encouraging this project and for bringing me together with my wonderful (and patient) agent Tim Brandhorst without whom this book would never have been created. I thank him for his wisdom, guidance, and clarity.

Thanks also go to the many students and colleagues whose life-journeys I've been privileged to be part of for more than 50 years. You have enriched my life.

My friends, both near and far, and those introduced via the technological ether, I thank you for your kind and thoughtful readings of my work and for your friendship and support. It has emboldened me.

To my generations upon generations of family now gone from this earthly realm, I thank you for the sacrifices and bravery and love of life that has given me such a rich bank of stories and has given me existence. To my extended family today, I thank you for your support and love which gives meaning to all I do. You will carry our shared stories forward.

To my daughter, Heather, and grandsons Miles and Jameson, all of whom bring the love of justice and caring into the world, I look forward to your future.

And, ultimately, to my husband John Baer, who has made our shared life better and richer and more glorious than any words could capture, I give my never-ending gratitude.

ABOUT THE AUTHOR

D r. Sylvia Baer is a professor of English at Rowan College, an Associate Fellow at Yale University (Davenport), and the Poet Laureate of Cape May, New Jersey, where her famed Poet-Tree blooms with poems each summer. She recently celebrated her fiftieth year of teaching. Contact Dr. Baer at www.sylviabaer.com or at sylviabaerwriter@gmail.com.

www.ingramcontent.com/pod-product-compliance
Lightning Source LLC
Chambersburg PA
CBHW071147130626
46553CB00004B/1555

9798986436111